Let Me Clear My Throat

LET ME CLEAR MY THROAT

ESSAYS

Elena Passarello

Sarabande ▓ Books

LOUISVILLE, KENTUCKY

Managing Editor
Sarabande Books, Inc.
2234 Dundee Road, Suite 200
Louisville, KY 40205

Library of Congress Cataloging-in-Publication Data

Passarello, Elena.
Let me clear my throat : essays / Elena Passarello. -- 1st ed.
    p. cm.
Includes bibliographical references.
ISBN 978-1-936747-52-8 (hardcover : acid-free paper) — ISBN 978-1-936747-45-0 (pbk. : acid-free paper) — ISBN 978-1-936747-50-4 (e-book)
I. Title.
PS3616.A856L48 2012
814'.6—dc23

                            2012011889

Cover and text design by Kirkby Gann Tittle.

This book is printed on acid-free paper.

Sarabande Books is a nonprofit literary organization.

This project is supported in part by an award from the National Endowment for the Arts.

The Kentucky Arts Council, the state arts agency, supports Sarabande Books with state tax dollars and federal funding from the National Endowment for the Arts.

For my family, the Passarellos, Hortons, and Turkels—

vibrant voices all.

CONTENTS

And Zeno was right to say that the voice was the flower of beauty.
—Michel de Montaigne,
"Apology for Raymond Sebond"

Let Me Clear My Throat

PART ONE

SCREAMING MEMES

Down in the Holler

HERE WE HAVE A FILM STILL OF BRANDO at his most filmable: garments rent and wet, hands cradling his temples, and the name of a star on his wide, taut lips. A half-dressed mass of wet sinew and moxie could keep any scene in the cultural memory, but "Stella!" would never be "Stella!" without Brando's gloriously ugly noise.

Most speech teachers will tell you the best way to tax your "instrument" is either to flatten the sound hole made by your lips, jaw, and throat or to finish your words in the rear of the mouth, rather than at the lips and front teeth. Throughout his movie career, Brando, the forebear of Mumblecore, rolled his voice toward his molars, where it slumped over his epiglottis like a delinquent schoolboy at the back of the bus. "Stella!" is no exception. That clenched neck squashes his airway, and his downturned mouth and retracted tongue reduce resonance. The bared teeth add grit and rape tone. If this voice had come from an inanimate instrument—a trombone, say—it would be one whose bell and slide had been run over by a streetcar.

This is not to say, however, that the "Stella!" could ever be improved upon, especially with something as Apollonian as voice training. Brando would add no further art to the moment by relaxing his throat and mouth into a broad and yawning "Stah-lah." In fact, an operatic "Stella!" might have made the sound forgettable, assuring it would never escape the world of the script. Brando's warped vocal channel—paired with a lung power as beefy as his young physique—shakes the boundaries of the context in which it is uttered, and takes it outside of the scene. This "Stella!" that we all remember is mighty, and it is mighty because it just *hurts*.

We hurt as he winces through the pained "Hey" and the bitten first vowel of her name. When he opens to that oft-mimicked, strained "aaaaugh," something gravelly and hoarse is hefted from within him, but can't quite make it out of his mouth, and that halted timbre hurts us, too. This transmutable hurt is what moves the line of dialogue to raw sound—what makes us hear the haggard notes of Brando's "Stella!" as a scream.

But what part of the scream moves us to keep referencing it? No other movie screams showed up a half-century later, in the mouths of *Seinfeld*'s Elaine Benes and *The Simpsons*' Ned Flanders. Though Brando yelled in *Julius Caesar* and *The Wild One*, those films' sounds weren't the grand finale of "Dueling Brandos," a *Saturday Night Live* skit that pitted Peter Boyle and John Belushi against each other, swapping "*Stella!*s" to the theme from *Deliverance*. And no other line of stage dialogue has been lauded in the style of the "Stella Shout Out," a twenty-six-year New Orleans tradition that invites contestants to try their best "Stella!" in Jackson Square.

But who wouldn't want to parrot a scream like "Stella!"? It's easy to learn, it's fun to scream, and it even gets a laugh, because screams like these hold special powers. "Stella!" is a screaming meme—a unit of vocal culture built to replicate and to travel. I submit that "Stella!" or any other scream with legs and momentum employs a three-ingredient recipe:

- It is physically impressive.
- It sounds out of place.
- It is somehow clownish.

It impresses us to watch the loose folds of Brando's T-shirt shake with his deep air. Such heavy sounds are periscopes from within the body, so much so that we the listeners consider this upheaval of lungs, organs, and muscles a corporeal gift. It also carries an impressively fearless and acrobatic physical artistry. Like watching a ballerina or an Olympic sprinter, this is a thrill we can take personally, because we are made of the same raw materials. Hearing Brando push his voice—an application nearly all of us are born with—suggests that inside *us* might be a "Stella!" that shakes the alleyways, especially because he uses that unprofessional throat shape to deliver the line. In doing so, he makes that much feeling look both cleansing and possible.

It sounds out of place because he is in the Faubourg Marigny at midnight, and, as Miz Eunice tells Stanley at the top of the scene, his kind of noise will force the law to "haul you in and turn the fire hose on you, like they did the last time." What's more, live man-screams were not common in early 1950s feature films. It was rare to see any A-list actor this loud, this up-close, and this unafraid to look shamefully desperate in a movie. Though we might now reward actors who immerse themselves so deeply in the muck of feeling, back then, it was not a part of filmmaking to watch them relinquish control to the camera. And this out-of-place-ness makes the scream doubly memorable.

And "Stella!" is clownish because the last syllable is a vomited, metallic duckwalk of a sound, more tenor than baritone, screamed by a man notorious for monkeying around with his voice (the cotton balls in *The Godfather*, the eerie drone of Kurtz, the show tunes in *Guys and Dolls*). It's clownish because only total clowns yell outside a girl's window and expect results. It's clownish because Brando played Stanley Kowalski as a goofy brute, perhaps to up the contrast between the character's resting self and his violent tendencies. And finally, it's clownish because, as cute as their intentions might be, clowns are also fucking terrifying.

But we must not forget that "Stella!" is also memorable because it *works*. Despite Stanley's rotten behavior in the scene before it, despite the weird and embarrassing sound that comes from his mouth, the camera cuts to a woman hearing his voice and then moving. She puts a zombie hand on the door and follows the sound down the wrought iron staircase, moving until she can find the body that screamed her name. Stella's palms sliding over that thorax that just trembled with sound; Stella's fingers caressing the wounded throat. Stella's calm and silent mouth sucking the fumes of the scream from the screamer.

Brando's "Stella!" says "I'm here," or "heal me," or perhaps "I will die if you do not come to me," and come Stella does. Perhaps we love "Stella!" because it is proof that the voice can move things in the outside world. That, in the body's arsenal, the voice can exist not as a genteel language delivery service, but as a means of control. "Stella!" proves that you might have wounded someone you love, you might have woken the neighbors, you might have pushed your voice until it sounds cartoonish and alien, but this scream of yours, if it comes from deep enough inside you, it is your best bet.

Perhaps this is the fourth tenet of my recipe for the screaming meme: at all costs, it must have the power to manipulate.

The Starlet

Now, Ann, in this one, you're looking down. When I start to crank, you look up slowly. You're quite calm; you don't expect to see a thing, then you just follow my directions. Alright? Camera! Look up slowly, Ann. That's it. You don't see anything. Now, look higher. Still higher.

Now, you see it! You're amazed! You can't believe it! Your eyes open wider. It's horrible, Ann, but you can't look away! There's no chance for you, Ann—no escape! You're helpless, Ann, helpless! You can't believe it!

There's just one chance—if you can scream. But your throat's paralyzed. Try to scream, Ann, try! Perhaps if you didn't see it, you could scream. Throw your arms across your eyes and scream, Ann, scream for your life!

The Wilhelm Scream

1951—EXT.—SWAMP—DAY

> The camera rolls. A PATSY stands waist-
> deep in a soundstage mock-up of Florida
> Alligator Water. You know the type: chicken
> eyes, hat askew, plywood gun.
>
> They never give guys like this a real gun.
>
> The water around him burbles. Something's
> got his right leg. The PATSY kicks that leg
> forward, throws back his hands, opens his
> mouth, and makes absolutely no noise.

MOST OF US TAKE OUR FIRST GULP OF AIR and immediately hurl it from our lungs in a scream. Perhaps this is a rejection of our initial breath; maybe it's a celebration of hitting the outside world with both lungs running. Regardless, from birth, our vocal cords work like fingerprints, telling the unique tales of our specific bodies. The sounds they make bounce around inside us and convert tones into nametags: Hello, my larynx is this large. Hello, my sinuses are stuffed with mucus. Hello, my diaphragm is stretched tight; listen to its shape as I spring air from it like a trampoline. Pleased to meet you.

Like breaking a box of emergency glass to pull an alarm, when we make our voices scream, the beeline of serious air not only buzzes the famous cords that create speech and song, it also crashes into a second pair of flaps at the top of the larynx: the false vocal cords. This creates the grate that we hear in a screamer's tone, a grate that articulates the rarity of its use. It says that a scream is physical work we should only force on ourselves at moments of ultimatum. That's why we know to come running when we hear a scream.

Storytelling complicates this physiological fact.

Imagine a quiet Warner Brothers sound studio in the dead of night. A man whose name we'll never know watches the dailies of the film *Distant Drums* in a cloud of cigarette smoke, warming up his voice and thinking of alligators. He's a looper, a vocal pro hired to redo every unmiked sound in the film: responses to punches, crowd gibber, barroom laughter. He studies the mouths of extras, like our condemned Patsy, so he can make sounds that match their faces. On the screen before him, the Patsy dies silently in the swamp, his mouth widened almost to a grin. The looper tries to mirror this strange gape and leans into the microphone. He inhales, closes his throat, and pushes out all the air that he had just pooled inside him. Up in the booth, an engineer corrals the session tape into a can, labeling it "MAN GETS EATEN BY ALLIGATOR."

Even without the sixty-year reputation and cultlike following that has eventually attached itself to this sound clip, "Man Gets Eaten by Alligator" is remarkable. It scrambles up the anonymous author's throat in an emasculating glissando, then slides back down the scale to land on a dejected "unh." Equal parts yelp, belch, and exhale, the scream is as dire as it is goofy, a buffet of all five falsetto vowels crashing into one another, then falling down a flight of stairs. On paper, it's impossible to render. My best guess would be: "IeehAAAA-OOUunh!"

"Hello, my leg is in the jaws of a gator," suggests the sound, but it also offers something more. There is no such thing as a "pure" recorded sound—one isolated from the myriad tones and white noise that surround every environment, even sound studios. Thus, as this man identifies himself through the resonance of his belly and throat, the doggedness of analog also captures the sound of that looping chamber. The buzz of the lights, the weight and tone of the conditioned air, even the whisper-thin curls from his cigarette all stow away on the ions that transfer to the tape. Thus, the reality of this original moment embosses itself in the reel along with the wavelengths of the scream. And though we audience members will hear the nameless screamer make this exact sound in this exact space at least two hundred times in the next half-century, we'll never be on a first-name basis with that original voice, that natural body, that primordial room.

```
CUT TO:
1953—EXT.—CHEYENNE COUNTRY

A posse of CAVALRY MEN rides through the
woods to save the kidnapped McKEEVER
SISTERS. As they enter enemy territory,
one soldier, WILHELM, lags behind.


               SGT. (shouting)

            Wilhelm! Wilhelm!



                  WILHELM

       Yeah, I'll just fill my pipe!
```

> CUE an onslaught of Cheyenne arrows, one
> of which hits WILHELM mid-thigh. WILHELM
> clutches his shot leg, opens his mouth.
>
> The sound of a man eaten by an alligator.

For many historians, filmmakers, and sound buffs, this is where it begins. Not with *Distant Drums,* the first film to use the scream, but with *Charge at Feather River*, where a named character—albeit an insignificant one—has the scream placed into his mouth. Hence, then and forever, "the Wilhelm Scream."

This film also marks the first use of the scream as horseplay; Wilhelm is not the only character who dies making the sound. Later in *Charge at Feather River*, a Cheyenne falls from a cliff while Wilhelm Scream-ing. A few scenes after this, a nameless soldier takes an arrow to the heart while making the same noise. Three sonically identical deaths in one film.

In these types of shoot-'em-ups, audiences expect a few dozen expendable deaths, be they in the bloodless Technicolor style of the 1950s. Perhaps the film was over budget and scrimped on sound; maybe the editing crew was too lazy to check for gaffes. But my hunch is that if you spend each day taping death knells and killing people off, you feel the urge to get creative. A body's got to have a little fun.

The scream is an off-camera nod between sound artists, who are as much patsies as any on-screen extra is. Their Wilhelm hijinks acknowledge, perhaps, the strange parameters of their nameless careers in the Hollywood system. A devious prank made even more devious because only those who know to listen for it will catch it. A middle finger right under the nose of the viewing public.

Imagine, months later, the *Charge at Feather River* debut at the Pantages. As always, the sound crew gets nosebleed seats. They watch Wilhelm shriek in pain, his larger-than-life eyes wide and pleading. As he screams that hysterical yelp, a smattering of ladies wince their sympathy for poor what's-his-name, and again, later for the other soldier guy, and maybe even later still for that injun fellow, while the soundmen around them all laugh like hell. Then they wonder what else they can get away with.

Two hundred films later, the answer is plenty.

```
CUT TO:
Present day—INT.—THE ANNALS OF FILM:

Hello my name is GUNMAN.
Hello my name is CREW MEMBER.
Hello my name is PASSERBY.
Hello my name is STORM TROOPER.
Hello my name is THE THIRD INDIAN.
Hello my name is MAD CHINAMAN.
Hello my name is HARADIM WARRIOR.
Hello my name is AN ENEMY SOLDIER.
                 A REBEL SOLDIER.
                 A NAZI SOLDIER.
Hello my name is DRUNKEN CARTEL HONCHO.
Hello my name is A CLOWN.
Hello my name is A MIME.
Hello my name is A CELLO PLAYER.
Hello my name is DUCK HUNTER.
Hello my name is MR. BROWN.
Hello my name is KUJO.
Hello my name is THUG #3.
Hello my name is VICTIM.
Hello my name is SOMEONE.
```

Does it relax us to watch these types of characters perish? Moments after the theater darkens, we assign our loyalty to the principals: leading man, comic relief, wise elder, character woman, wacky best friend. Those headliners are our kin. We then prove kinship by treating extras and day-players like outsiders. Nameless henchmen are folks to whom we don't send Christmas cards. Hard luck vagabonds are the kind of people we pass on the street without greeting. Sometimes the relief of watching the anonymous die, because of the knowledge that they aren't "ours," is so palpable that we laugh with gratitude.

```
CUT TO: 1954—INT.—A RUN-DOWN SHACK

JAMES WHITMORE is trying his damnedest
to stay caught in the unconvincing
death-grip of a GIANT ANT. He turns his
face from camera, perhaps to tell the
ANT PUPPETEER to tighten his hold on
WHITMORE'S SQUIRMING TORSO, or else the
scene will look more ridiculous than it
already does. WHITMORE grips the GIANT
ANT'S mandibles and flexes. Regardless
of what his obscured mouth is actually
doing, he screams for his life.
```

When Puccini throws Tosca from her tower, he gives her cushions of vowels to land on:

O Scarpia, avanti a Dio!

These ten syllables are as wide open and as pure a series of sounds as a body can make, the rush of well-rounded air stopped by only a muted smattering of consonants. Thus, each and every Tosca dies with her soft palate lifted and her diaphragm flexed like a bicep.

The big names of Shakespeare die on rounded whole notes as well. Many of his title characters sound death alarums with mouths like egg cups:

Hamlet, in the Bad Quarto: *O O O O*.
Othello, in the bedroom: *O O O*.
Lear, after the undoing of his top button: *O O O*.

Even Falstaff gets into the act, after half of Windsor attacks him with tapers, one easy-on-the-throat O for each excruciatingly silly poke. The reason for this is, of course, protection. As Tosca, Maria Callas launched her last words around the globe, evenings and matinees, for most of her adult life. As the Moor, David Garrick howled over his fake stab wound for decades. Human throats, no matter how well-oiled, can't take the stress of screaming the sounds of the dying.

Regular speech, like the vowels above, sends a sweet spurt of air up the trachea. When it meets the two vocal cords, they're ready for it, bussing each other while they wait. A scream's rush of unplanned, unsupported air is too heavy for the cords to endure. Blown back from their gentle position, they stretch unnecessarily or overextend, causing tissue to warp and swell. Imagine running a marathon with no training, and how wobbly you'd walk for the next week or so. That's one night of hard screaming at, say, a playoff game, after which your voice is hoarse for forty-eight hours. Now imagine running that marathon again and again, never stretching, never hydrating. That's vocal damage, where the repeated strain of unbalanced air actually causes calluses—called nodules—to harden onto the vocal cords, preventing them from ever closing as prettily as they once did. This injury is a bankable one for few performers, maybe Rod Stewart or Harvey Fierstein. Puccini and Shakespeare must both have known that tragic heroes with throat barnacles couldn't sell tickets.

When my friend Jeffrey had to play a man howling over the corpse of his brother, he trained for the event like a laryngeal body-builder. "I knew that I had to let out this yell every night, so, at that point, basically, [the scream] was an exercise—really using the diaphragm and my breath to get the sound out safely," he remembers. "I didn't have the context of the scene in my mind at all." Instead, he pictured the same image Olivier did when playing Oedipus—an arctic ermine whose tongue had frozen to a salt lick trap. "I used that for the feeling of being totally stuck. Completely powerless," he says.

The run of this play was short enough for Jeffrey to take some physical risks with his scream. Though he supported his voice, he let the audience have it. When he screamed in that big warehouse theater space, people jumped. They thought his sound was recorded. Because only in canned sounds, like those in the movies, can a listener be treated to something that spot-on in one take. Only in films do we get to hear something that "real."

```
CUT TO:
1954—INT.—A WELL-APPOINTED LIVING ROOM

"You know, I get pretty girlish in this
number," beams JUDY GARLAND as she spins
around her Malibu home. She's playing a
film starlet goofing around to a soundtrack
record on her hi-fi. Her husband, JAMES
MASON, ogles her as she pulls an epic
Hollywood number out of thin air. This
is the magic we expect from America's
sweetheart, who needs only a few
household props, her big eyes, and her
even bigger voice to sell a song.

Hello, my name is unsinkable pluck.

The soundtrack record is a sonic tour-of-
nations. For a verse scored as a French
can-can, GARLAND high-kicks, squeezing
a throw pillow like an accordion. For
```

```
a section scored in samba, GARLAND
wields salt shakers like maracas. Spooky
"Transylvania" music plays as she creeps
across the floor.

That's when Garland mounts the fireplace
mantel and strikes a pose, and the record
plays that SCREAM: just as loud, just as
anguished, just as primal as it was in
WILHELM'S Wild West.

GARLAND poses through the resting
measure. MASON leers, smoking and
slurring. Neither lover seems surprised
to hear the SCREAM. This is, after all,
Hollywood.
```

It's with this film that the Wilhelm Scream gets interesting. We're not on the lonesome trail, in the Everglades, or seconds away from being mutant ant food. We're indoors. If the scream belongs anywhere in this picture, it's at the end, when Mason's character drowns himself. Instead, in that scene, we watch a soundless, buttery-soft death: Mason walking solemnly into the Malibu sunset. We know he's gone not from hearing a scream, but from seeing his unmanned cabana robe floating in the seaweed.

In the actual scene with the scream, Mason is alive and convivial; he and Garland are newlyweds eating sandwiches, singing and necking and bouncing the light of their star power off each other's foreheads. Using the Wilhelm here—in a *musical number*, no less— is like putting the scream on top of a chocolate sundae.

But look again. Judy Garland (*née* Frances Ethel Gumm) was 31 when she played 22-year-old Mrs. Norman Maine (*née* Esther Blodgett), but she looked at least 40. Her skin was dull from pills, two nervous breakdowns, and liquor. The Assistant Director's report lists clockwork "sick days": *Nov. 9, 10, 11, 12, 19, 20, 21; Dec. 21, 22; Jan. 16, 21, 29; Feb. 6, 10, 19, 22, 26: Judy was ill and did not work. March 5, 8: Judy went home; too tired to work. March 16: Judy left the lot to go to the doctor. April 19, 20, 21, 22, 23, 24: Judy was ill and could not make post-recordings. Judy taking time off to rest.*

Delivery boys arrived on motorcycles from five separate pharmacies carrying Seconal, Dexamyl, the paraldehyde that made her smell so bad the makeup girls were loath to touch her. Still, everyone interviewed about the harried making of *A Star Is Born* agrees that, whenever Cukor yelled "Action," Garland plowed through each scene like a prizefighter. Right past the camera, a psychiatric nurse posing as a "personal secretary" waited to actually catch her in between takes. And nearly all those takes were fantastic.

Even though in many ways the use of the scream in *A Star Is Born* is the most laughable, in some ways it's the most accurate, as well as the most important. Thanks to this film, we hear the famous death scream in tandem with an image of an actual dying person: by the end of the decade, Garland's liver will all but completely shut down and doctors will pump twenty quarts of fluid from her body. How could any shiny-faced day player with a trick arrow in his leg manage a better on-screen death scene? And what vowels could Shakespeare possibly string together to render this kind of life-or-death tension?

Not to mention, the sound engineers placed the scream in the song break—a moment of total silence. No hoof-beats, gunshots, or weather sounds were blended into it. It's also untainted by scoring or Foley effects, and all this makes it the purest appearance of the scream in film history. Because of this, in the late twentieth century, when Lucas, Tarantino, and Jackson included the scream in their films as homage, it's likely they pirated the bite from this film and not from a master reel.

It's probably a clip from *A Star Is Born* that we hear in the *Lord of the Rings* and *Star Wars* trilogies. Judy's Wilhelm Scream in *Reservoir Dogs*, Judy in *Spaceballs*. Judy in *Get Rich or Die Tryin'* and Judy in *Kung Fu Panda*. Judy in *Planet of the Apes*. Judy in *Howard the Duck*.

```
CUT TO:
1969—EXT.—A MEXICAN SOUNDSTAGE

What's a goofy scream like Wilhelm's
doing in a movie with close-ups on exit-
wounds and hundreds of gallons of blood
packs?

25 people die in the first action sequence
alone; TEMPERANCE WOMEN are trampled by
horses; three TOWNSPEOPLE take bullets in
the time it takes an OUTLAW's corpse to
fall from the Post Office roof.

A RANDOM HORSEMAN rides into the fray.
CUT to a GUNMAN firing. CUE the SCREAM,
its power blended into a blur of camera
motion. CUT back to the HORSEMAN in
close-up, clutching his bleeding eye. His
hand covers his forehead; his death now
faceless as well as nameless.

When you put the SCREAM this way, maybe
it actually could be scary.
```

Soon after that theater gig that required him to scream daily onstage, my friend Jeffrey found an occasion to scream for real. One chilly May dawn, his house caught fire, forcing both him and his girlfriend to jump, naked, from their second-story window and watch the place burn down before fire trucks arrived. It took less than a half hour for Jeffrey to scream himself hoarse, damaging his well-trained vocal cords into silence for a full week. Only a heavy-duty injection of cortisone brought any sound back and, four and a half years later, he says he still hasn't totally healed. It was the first time in his life he ever screamed without thinking about it first.

When I showed up at his house, about an hour after he jumped, Jeffrey was quiet. He paced the crusts of his property, wrapped in an oversized blanket, staring upward with red, dry eyes. He rasped, "Oh God. Oh God," until his voice waned and eventually slipped away, as if spiraling down a wet well. And then he was just mouthing the words.

Like the Patsy, slipping into the green swamp water, forbidden to make a noise.

Like the woman on the beach one summer vacation whom we watched as a dozen men pulled her bloated, blue husband from the Florida undertow. For the hour it took to get him back on the sand, she gripped a lifeguard, swallowing all the air as if to hoard it. Instead of exhaling, her mouth hung uselessly. Her slack jaw tipped forward to her concave torso, which jerked inward with each gulp of soundless breath.

She sucked the sound out of the periphery. The whistles of the lifeguard, the crunch of ambulance tires on the sand, and the swollen tide all leapt into her heaving mouth. Then, when she'd finished eating sound, she inhaled the ridiculous beach tchotchkes around her, muting the green frogs that danced over her maillot, the graying red swim trunks and rainbow towels and SpongeBob shovels and whale-shaped buckets. And then she said something.

Her husband's body now black-and-white, she stood four paces from him, the joints of her knees and elbows pointing to opposite ends of the shore. She peered into the lifeguard's reflector shades and, like a bad actress, ended each whispered syllable with a full stop: "I. Need. You. To. Tell. Me. It's. Going. To. Be. O. K."

```
CUT TO:
2006—MONT.—A FICTITIOUS LOBBYIST
MONOLOGUES ABOUT A COLLEAGUE
```

                    NICK NAYLOR (V.O.)

```
After watching the footage of the Kent
State shootings, Bobby Jay, then 17,
signed up for the National Guard so that
he, too, could shoot college students.
But the National Guard recruiter was out
to lunch, so Bobby Jay ended up shooting
Panamanians instead. Which is almost as
good as college students, only they shoot
back.
```

A few weeks ago, I identified a Wilhelm on my own for the first time, and it made me feel like a birder spotting rare fowl in the woods without a guidebook. I had rented the satire of Big Tobacco, *Thank You for Smoking*, which fires the scream within the first ten minutes of the film. When I thought I'd heard it, I reversed the video several times, playing a few frames again and again to make sure. The scream was well buried in Foley and soundtrack, but it was there. The first time Wilhelm ever waved at me and I had the chance to wave back.

Nobody really dies in *Thank You for Smoking*. The Wilhelm occurs during a sort of flashback scene in which three pieces of archival footage are welded together and underscored by Aaron Eckhart's narration: first, a wide shot of the Kent State Commons, dotted with a thousand Guardsmen and their gear. Then a closer shot of the troops marching with gas-masked heads turned toward the camera. Then a final shot of a tear-gas bomb firing, trailing smoke on its way to a running man in plain clothes. He ducks, but the footage is too grainy to tell whether or not his mouth is open. Cue the scream.

I imagined another sound studio, this time, a digital one. A sound editor watches a rough cut of the film and decides that Nick Naylor's Kent State monologue, when accompanied with the historical footage that the director insisted on, is too harsh, even for black comedy.

He watches the bomb head straight for the brow of a single student and he winces. Shit, he thinks, I've got to lighten this up. Make a joke out of this ducking kid and the whole old, dead event. I need something to remind the audience that it's only a movie. I need something to make it less real.

The Motor-Mouth

*Your filler words have got to be easy, with no chop.
You can't pick words with hard endings, because you
can't have anything in your chant that makes you stop
and start. Like, in "do it," that T is a stopping point in
sound; it's very hard to go from "iT" to "three-dollar
bid."*

*I use "dollar-dollar," "look-a-them," "look-at-them-
right-there," "put-them-on-the-money," "how-many-
dollars-on-them." After you say them long enough, your
tongue does like a blend of all the words, so "you-ought-
to-give" sounds more like "yadagivadagivadagiv." Some
people pick it up really fast, but it took me, I'd say, six
months before I was able to feel like I could get up and
not embarrass myself. I practiced in the car every day—
driving down the road and selling the telephone poles.*

*Once you get the chant, there's a lot of subliminal things
you can do with the crowd. You ask in tens and chant
through ten, twenty, thirty, up to a hundred, and when
you get a hundred-dollar bid, you go up a half-step,
like a key change. And that changes the mood and the
excitement of the whole room.*

*There was one charity auction over in South Africa
where I sold a piece of real estate for twenty-eight-point-
five million. And I had started at nine million. As I hit
twelve, then fifteen, then seventeen, the crowd would*

cheer more, and I'd raise my pitch up and up, and then finally when I said SOLD!, the whole place just exploded in applause. I mean exploded.

It gives you a mix of feelings. You're so nervous for the buyer and the seller, because there's so much at stake for them with an item that big. But you're loving being the performer as well. You get a tingling feeling in your stomach as you're looking at the crowd. But you aren't thinking about your voice, really. Your mouth is just going—it's almost as if you're watching yourself do it. I suppose you could call it surreal.

How to Spell the Rebel Yell

"Yee-aay-ee!"
— Margaret Mitchell

"Wah-Who-Eeee!"
— Chester Goolrick

"Rrrrrr-yahhhhhhhhhhhhhhhhhhh-yip-yip-yip-yip-yip!"
— H. Allen Smith

"More! More! More!"
— Billy Idol

FIRST MANASSAS. IN THE NINETY-DEGREE HEAT, the Union fords Bull Run and busts through line after line of Confederate troops, aiming for the railroad to Richmond. Under the grassy shield of Henry House Hill's western slope, the Confederates scramble for reinforcements. Somebody overhears Brigadier General Bee comparing Brigadier General Jackson to a "stone wall." This is said to either compliment Jackson's steadfastness or jeer his languor. No one will ever know for certain, since Bee is shot dead shortly after the quip leaves his lips.

The voices of war can turn gossip into nicknames, dialogue into mythology. And Lord only knows what parts of any war story are actually true. At Manassas, folks just take what they think they overhear Bee saying and run with it.

"Stonewall" Jackson runs as well. He turns away from Bee and charges up Henry House Hill with his 4th Virginia infantrymen, pausing before reaching the top. His whole brigade is about to come nose-to-nose with the Union, but first he turns back to them, raising a hand to God. Pipe down, the troops tell each other. He's going to say something to us. The General opens his mouth.

·

To hear Walt Whitman tell it, a war can begin and end with voices. Whitman's first memory of the secession is walking down Broadway in the early hours of April 13, 1861, as the cries of the newsboys precede their physical approach. First yells, then young footsteps, then their words in soprano: "tearing and yelling up the street, rushing from side to side even more furiously than usual."

Later into the night, under the gas lamps of the Metropolitan Hotel, only a few patrons, Whitman included, carry a copy of that Extra in their vest pockets. Voices hush to murmurs as one person reads the facts of the war aloud: "All listen'd silently and attentively," Whitman says. "No remark was made by any of the crowd, which had increas'd to thirty or forty, but all stood a minute or two, I remember, before they dispers'd."

It is a careful business, wrapping words around these kinds of moments—moments of unintelligible volume, or of silence, or of lost dialogue. All three are charged with an emotion that can't be recounted from a seated position, but Whitman does it. He quotes neither the newsboys nor the voice reading the papers, but, in his account, both feel audible. We force his words, which stand as both a buffer and a conduit, to carry added sound.

There is sound in the words Whitman uses, like "loud" and "cries." Sound in "crowd" and sound in "silently." And even sound in words that aren't about noise—verbs like "rushing," nouns like "midnight," proper nouns like "Broadway," adverbs like "furiously."

This is the sound of "furiously": little heels spinning circles in the dirt, pivoting between the pedestrians, changing directions.

•

On the backside of Henry House Hill, Stonewall Jackson's low growl carries. He tells his men to hold fire until they're close enough to bayonet, and the lot of them lurches upward. Shelby Foote imagines Jackson then telling his men to "yell like furies," but legend implies that he says something closer to "yell like we practiced!" This command would support the theory that the collective sound erupting from the mouths of the Stonewall Brigade is a dictated, spellable thing. A line to memorize, like "Attack!" or "Hut-Hut-Hike!"

It would also confirm that, somewhere between mustering up at Harpers Ferry and crossing the bridge at Bull Run, the 4th Virginia had rehearsed their war cry, their world-famous polar opposite to the "hip-hip-huzzah!" that Jackson learned at West Point. It would prove that there was method to the unexpected sound that some say shifted this battle's advantage to the Confederates. It would validate the notion that, yes, a soldier's throat hits specific notes when it sings of brutality, and Stonewall Jackson—silent, biblical, obsessive—was just the man to score them into a particular order and cadence.

Muskets quiet, they all tip over the hill, bridging the gap between their guns and the enemy with sound. It is the first major battle of the first and only War Between the States, and the first recorded appearance of the yell. About the time Jackson's men run down the hill, the remaining Union troops—exhausted, confused and ill-informed—back the hell away from that sound and from its corporeal presence.

The Union retreat is called "The Great Skedaddle." The Southern war cry is called "the Pibroch of the Confederacy."

Or, if you are Indiana Lieutenant Ambrose Bierce, "The ugliest sound that any mortal ever heard."

Or, if you are Stonewall Jackson, "The sweetest music I ever heard."

•

Four years later, Whitman hears tell of Sherman's troops, after the fire, hanging a left at Savannah. When they receive the news of Appomattox, these Union soldiers yell for miles; they yell across two Carolinas, necks straining toward the Mason-Dixon like horses that can see the barn. Whitman rewords the sonic moment twenty years after the fact: "at intervals all day long sounded out the wild music of those peculiar army cries."

No one cared to investigate the exact shape of this joyful Union yell—the placement of the palate, the pitch or the rhythm or the phonemes. We're happy to hear from Whitman that, just like in his account of the newsboys or the hotel recitation, voices sounded and those voices eventually stopped.

Sometimes, however, a vocal moment is not so lucky.

Why can we let some parts of history live locked in the figurative, while insisting that others be specified? Why can we hear The Shot Heard 'Round the World without spending centuries wondering what it sounded like, desperate to know for certain whether Charleston shook with a "Boom," a "Thud," or a "Ker-blam?"

•

"The Southern soldiers cannot cheer," writes a London *Times* reporter called William Howard Russell in 1861. "What passes muster for that jubilant sound is a shrill ringing scream with a touch of the Indian war-whoop in it." Russell is one of the five hundred civilians—dozens of them politicians—who plan a picnic on the riverbank to watch what was forecast to be a swift Union victory. Most sit idly as their picnic morphs into a long, loud battle with a panicked finale, but fifty or so of the group make their way even closer to the battlefield so that, when the bridge falls, they are trapped on the wrong riverbank alongside the fleeing Union soldiers. Russell and four senators are among these fifty, all of whom are probably within earshot of that first concentrated Confederate yell.

Shortly thereafter, descriptions of the yell begin appearing in British newspapers, publishing houses, and women's magazines. The English, and not the Americans, are who give the yell its first mythic punch. Englishwoman Catherine C. Hopely publishes an account of First Manassas, noting that a particular "shout of triumph" made the Union soldiers "overpowered by terror. One frightened company infected the rest, and the result is known." Officer Fitzgerald Ross tells *Blackwood's Magazine* that the cry is a "terrible scream...a real Southern yell which rang along the whole [Confederate] line" and could be heard "a mile off." Bell Irwin Wiley takes a recipe approach: "It had in it a mixture of fright, pent-up nervousness, exultation, hatred and a pinch of pure deviltry."

The Brits are even the ones who give the yell its name. British officer and military reporter Arthur Fremantle notes in *Three Months in the Southern States* that "the Rebel yell has a particular merit, and always produces a salutary and useful effect upon their adversaries." To him, the yell of the rebels sounds more like an expression of "delight." Other dispatches treat the newly named Yell as if it is a kind of modern weaponry, a technological advancement on a par with the Williams Breech-loading Rapid Fire Gun, or Professor

Thaddeus Lowe's *Enterprise*, the hot-air balloon commissioned by the Union for scouting. Other times, the Yell is spotted like rare birdsong, at Chancellorsville, at Lovejoy Station, at Chickamauga, at Second Manassas.

Several dozen of these later reports use feminine words to describe the cry, calling it "shrill" or "shrieking" or "womanish." Some compare it to the sound of a rabbit in mortal peril. But in reality, the cry reflects the particular perils of marching in a Confederate line. Lumped into companies with mismatched uniforms, their soldiers hadn't the luxury of standing in Academy ranks and learning how to plant their feet, how to fortify the voice with the diaphragm and let loose an earthy "Huzzah!"

The West Point huzzah that the Union still carries is much more rightfully called a yell: forceful, loud, and well-supported. It ends on a stretchable vowel, the mouth relaxed and haughty. But the Yell, at least in the eyes of the descriptive Brits, is wilder—why else would they compare it to funeral mourners, to defenseless bunnies, or to "the weaker sex?" Perhaps they do this because the sounds of the Yell are those of perceived victimhood. And how might a well-trained soldier attack a "victim" who screams as he approaches, bayonet at the ready?

In a way, screaming is biologically designed to support this muddled expectation. In order to be effective, a huzzahlike yell must speak of a specific, confident place, but a scream must appear *out* of place. The violent rush of terrified air finds unexpected pockets of the throat and mouth to inhabit. Fear lifts the palate and quickens the speed of exhalations, raising the pitch so that it cuts through the noise of cannon fire and horses to locate help. A scream is, essentially, the sound of the self trying to move when its body cannot run away.

•

Imagine watching Jackson's men emerge from the smoke, zooming toward you as if pulled on dollies. Their mouths and teeth are black from biting off the tops of their gunpowder cartridges, and those smeared black mouths are wet and open. They sing like very frightened things, underscoring their fight with the sounds of flight. As they halve the distance between you and them, you know that this is the space of time you should devote to firing or running. Instead, you find yourself staring, thinking.

Lord in heaven, you say to nobody in particular. How does a body go about attacking a bunch of freaks like these?

And then, to your left, there is William Russell on the crumbling bridge, pen in hand, watching your unwounded Union fellows leap into hospital carts and cower. Perhaps he, in turn, wonders, "How can I possibly put this on paper so that nobody will forget it?"

·

When the nineteenth century rolls into the twentieth, Rebel Yell detectives become less interested in describing the Yell and more interested in spelling it. This happens at the same time that many Confederate veterans publish memoirs, and also as the Civil War becomes a go-to setting for popular fiction and film. There is a spelled-out Yell in *Gone with the Wind*. The mad preacher in *Light in August* hears one. Retired Colonel Harvey Dew spells it "Woh-who—ey! who—ey! who—ey," offering step-by-step instructions in *Century Illustrated Magazine*: "sound the first syllable 'woh' short and low, and the second 'who' with a very high and prolonged note deflecting upon the third syllable 'ey.'" There is no record of *Century Illustrated*'s subscribers practicing the Yell at home.

In 1952, Yankee humorist H. Allen Smith drives south on the *Saturday Evening Post*'s dime. Once he crosses the Mason-Dixon, he begins asking "experts" in several states to Yell for him, hoping to land on a unified, spellable sound to add to the American lexicon. The war is almost a century old, barely a shadow in the living memory. Many aspects of both the fighting and the whole of the Antebellum South have already dissolved into paraphrase, or worse, into the funhouse mirror of hyperbole. "On the brash assumption that there is going to be a posterity," Smith writes, "I believe that posterity will be immensely curious about this matter."

Commonalities of spelling aren't easy to come by. According to Smith, the Yell of the Charleston lawyer ("Yuhhhhhh-wooooo-ooooooo-eeeeeeeeeeeeeee-UH!") is spelled differently from that of the Virginia historian ("Yeeeeeeeeeeee-ahhhhhhhhhhhhhh-hhhhhh!") or the Chapel Hill partygoer ("Whoooooooooooooooo-wow!").

Perhaps, then, there never really was a unified Yell, just a few hundred thousand Southern troops opening their mouths and letting rip the loudest sounds they could stomach. This would render the Rebel babble more like Babel. But Smith presses on, adapting his short article into a book, refusing to admit that no one real sound ever existed. Because where's the fun in that?

A newspaperman in Virginia Beach offers Smith another take on the Yell, insisting that it is merely one representative of a universally understood battle cry: "The Persians yelled the rebel yell at Thermopylae and the Spartans yelled the rebel yell right back at them. The British grenadiers yelled it at Balaklava and the Russians screeched it back. The communists in Korea today are yelling it at us, and we are not answering with mumbles. . . . You know very well that if a wave of our boys came charging across the fields, shrieking the rebel yell, the Yankees didn't greet them with silence."

•

Back at Bull Run, the Union troops are dehydrated and exhausted from a twenty-mile walk in wicked heat. It's already four o'clock, and they haven't won yet. Many of them were told this war wouldn't last more than two months. Now they're knee-deep in cannon smoke, shooting their own men because they can't distinguish between the gray of their enemy's uniforms and the blue of their own. They stand on the other side of Henry House Hill, yelling.

"Betrayed!" they say, shooting the sound toward their fellow officers, at God, at the rich picnickers they spot in the distance. A few hours later, they break formation and run back to Washington, yelling together once again. William Howard Russell calls them "a shouting, screaming mass of men on foot, who were literally yelling with rage." One would presume that this kind of rage also cannot be spelled. But for some reason, these yells are much less famous.

•

Two years after the death of the last Civil War veteran, linguist Allen Walker Reed publishes an article in *American Speech* that makes a case for the Rebel Yell as a "linguistic problem," one that looks so ugly in written form because it lives outside the conventional parameters of language. "The syllables found in words like *hip, huzzah, hooray* clearly fall within the pattern of English," Reed says. "The same can be said of the college yells of the present day, as in 'Bocka-wocka-choom; bocka-wocka-cha; bocka-wocka, chocka-wocka, sis-boom-bah.'" The Yell, however, while just as nonsensical as a fight song, doesn't mimic any established consonant-vowel pairings. In a five-part proof of the Yell as an anomaly, Reed calls it "a total organismic response" that "completed the full involvement of the whole soldier."

"I believe," he says, "that the true rebel yell occurred only under the excitement and tension of the battlefield, and therefore the real thing has not been heard since 1865." Reed's treatise, however, doesn't stop historians, reenactors, and linguists from trying to capture the Yell. They vow to trap it—an auditory lightning bug in a jar—straight into the digital age.

•

Of the three known recordings of Confederates rebel-yelling, two now live online. Of these, one bite is partially the work of reenactors, who, after a few jovial "Hoot-hoo-hoo-hoo's," giggle at each other. "At'suh Ribble Yill! Hee-hee-heee!" says a creaky voice close to the microphone. He sounds more like a cartoon prospector than a soldier. No one would ever turn tail for this uninspired whooping. Still, this is the same clip that appears in Ken Burns' documentary on the war, and for that reason, many take this Yell as gospel. Its competitor is a single-voiced Yell by Thomas Alexander, a veteran of the 37th North Carolina, who removed his dentures before yelling in a Charlotte radio studio in 1935. This sound, high in pitch and very unspellable, is strange and decidedly fiercer: a kelpie having a 100-decibel asthma attack.

Regardless of whether these recorded throats served any real time on American battlefields, no geriatric veteran, with his stringy diaphragm and arid larynx, can make the same sound as a pink-lunged boy in 1861. Further, no resting body reverberates the same way as a body barreling downhill—heart bursting, tongue rotting in powder, carrying both itself and the nation into a new kind of warfare for the very first time.

After hearing these two clips, it is easy to put to bed the possibility of the Yell ever living on.

But for countless Americans, the sound does not disappear when the Civil War falls further behind us; it lives on in a different kind of fighting. Many of us hear the phrase "rebel yell" and think only of civilians: of mobs violating captive and outnumbered bodies, bodies that are not made fair game through a military contract. Scholar and statesman James Weldon Johnson, who coined the soldering phrase "Red Summer" to describe the season in which fifty black citizens were lynched in towns from Bisbee to Charleston to Chicago to DC, heard the Yell this way. In his novel *Autobiography of an Ex-Colored Man*, the protagonist encounters a crowd of white citizens "emitting that . . . rebel yell" while they burn a black man in a Jacksonville town square. The narrator does not parse out the sound, or give hints as to its pitch or rhythm. He only describes it as "terror-inducing."

But there is sound buried in the typeface of "terror-inducing," though the specific reverberations might change from reader to reader. "Terror-inducing" is a cry of the unspeakable, the unsound-able. It is the sound of a volatile bunch so agitated with sinister energy that none can predict what the group is capable of. By making this the only vocal description in an otherwise exhaustively depicted scene, Johnson proves that a sound which induces terror is a sound that cannot be mapped.

The off-the-charts sound that rings in Johnson's scene speaks to a dumbfounding magic, the limbic trickery that allows a long-dead (if ever-lived) sound to underscore a documented atrocity. Here, we see how wording can allow a shout that decayed with the mouths of the 4th Virginia to live, serving as a fight song for our most indelible domestic terrorisms. This places the Yell here in Johnson's novel, and in similarly savage locations throughout the twentieth century. For many, the Yell stops not with the death of the last Johnny Reb, but with this—a sound as nebulous and unheard as the shouts at Bull Run, but also every bit as loud.

•

But what makes the magic of "rebel yell" even more confounding is that, in the past fifty years, the phrase has also transported itself to a second, equally divergent place, a flip and funky place, one as far from First Manassas as from the town square in Johnson's novel.

For many, the phrase has moved away not just from carnage, but from sound altogether—immigrating to art house marquees, or streetwise clothing lines, or Nevada college newspaper mastheads, or roller coasters, or rock and roll.

"Rebel yell" has proven consistently catchy, as it hasn't left the pop culture vocabulary in 150 years. So perhaps it's neither phonemes nor volume that keeps the pop public's interests. Maybe the sound of the *phrase* "rebel yell" is what draws us in. Maybe the true magician of the Yell is not Jackson, but Arthur Fremantle, who left Manassas, went home, and wrote a perfect piece of speech to describe a cry that can't be typeset. This would help explain how, on the sesquicentennial of Bull Run, the words "rebel yell" have overtaken the historical point of origin.

Just reading the phrase "rebel yell" requires a lively motion. When it is typed out, the reader's eyes leapfrog from vowel to vowel, hurdling over the tall stems of each consonant. And when voiced, those consonants pool both air and tone in the front of the mouth. They are revved by the opening *r*, volleyed back by the *b*. The *y* boomerangs that last, perfect short *e* to the lips, and the low-growled double *l* coaxes it right back, cocking the mouth. The phrase has the same rhythm as themes from Mozart and the gallop of hoofbeats. Does any gibbered, culturally complex war cry deserve a name that's so fun to say?

Culture now embraces the term "rebel," once entirely pejorative. After all, Bob Marley pooled some of the best noises a human could make into an album called *Rebel Music*. And it can't be a coincidence that the Hamburglar, the coolest character ever to peddle fast food, says "robble robble." And who in their right minds wants to imagine Billy Idol singing about a "babe" who, "in the midnight hour," cried "more, more, more" with a "Yankee Huzzah?"

Now, when I imagine a "rebel" on the banks of Bull Run, James Dean is there: a civilian redcoat. I see David Bowie's hot tramp riding the Bull Run bridge in a torn, tacky dress, drinking a glass of bottom-shelf gutter bourbon and yelling along with the thousands of soldiers.

She yells, "He's a rebel and he'll never-never be any good." She yells, "Hey-hey-hey! I was born a rebel! With one foot on the grave and one foot on the pedal." She yells, "A cell is hell; I'm a rebel so I rebel." For fifty years' worth of pop vocals, she yells and yells and yells.

•

And with that second word of the perfect phrase, "yell," comes an even larger army, bookending the soldiers of First Manassas by millennia. Cresting Henry House Hill, behind Jackson's men, behind the screaming, resurrected body of General Bee, comes Diomedes of the Loud War Cry, his armor ringing out in sounds that are fifteen syllables long. Shakespeare's Troilus chases him, shouting a war cry of his own: "O false Cressid! False, false, false!" And behind them come epochs of soldiers—bleeding, yelling, running, firing, misunderstanding each other.

The Kamikazes yell "Tiger! Tiger! Tiger!" in the roar of the radio signal "Tora," and their countrymen fill "Banzai" with the sound of ten thousand years. A celestial army evokes the name of their dragon-slayer, either as a moniker, "He Who Resembles God," or as a question, "Who is like God?" In either case, their noise is heard as "Michael."

The Finns yell "Fire at their balls!" while the Saxon fyrd yells "Out, Out, Out!" The Calvary, never ones for subtlety, just yell "Charge!" Then the Swedes yell "Cut Them Down!" as the Czechs yell "At Them!" and their syllables are nearly identical to each other. A wall of Argentine sailors yells "Ura!" while the Bulgarians yell "Ure"; the Serbs yell "Urah" and our Marines "Ooo-ruh": all of them prompts for their enemies' bodies to rid themselves of the air in their lungs.

And the Athenians shout "Eleleu," which is how Greek owls like to hoot. Because, whether *cocorico* or *cockadoodledo*, the sun might not rise on them the next morning.

And when wounded, they all yell *Ow! Joj! Array! Oof! Aix! Au! Auwa! Ack!* and *¡Uy!* before they hit the earth. Because, "Mayday" or *M'aidez*, theirs are the planes most likely to tip downward.

The Candidate

In a race for mayor, you'll speak for a filled auditorium, and the same day you'll be in living rooms with twelve people. And then there are debates; in the end we did thirty-eight. And our campaign stressed a strong field effort, so we were also going door to door. And, of course, you need to be on the phone. It ends up being over twelve hours each day for ten weeks—ten weeks of speaking.

When you're running for office, you're often stopping at places where there isn't a sound system. So I lost my voice a bunch. One night ended at an event at the Beehive on the South Side, and it was packed. I was standing on a chair, and to be heard from the back of that room all the way to the curb, the only option was to scream.

I started getting coaching from local actors—you know, lemon juice, gargling with salt water—but there were several times when I would say, "I can't talk anymore. It just hurts." But a good staff is very unsympathetic. They just give you hot tea and say, "You only have thirty-five days until this is over. Your hurt voice isn't enough to change the schedule."

I think I was born with a passion to do my job and that comes through in my speaking. I think it helps that I don't have a "professional" voice—I have a little twang of a Pittsburgh accent. I'm very sensitive to BS, too. I know I would rather hear the monotone voice of someone with conviction than the impassioned voice of a fake. On the other hand, you don't want to come off as a robot. It's a very delicate line, to show that you are a human being, but not go so far that someone might question your competence.

I'm only worried about getting in a situation where I just freeze. I don't prepare my speeches beforehand—I just plan in my head, you know, "These are the four things I'm going to say out there." And I'm afraid of the one time when I'll get up there and I'll be like, "Oh shit, what was number two?" It hasn't happened yet, but I'm assuming it will one day, because of the law of averages. I just hope that, at the point where it happens, I can be funny, 'cause being funny's your only option at that point.

Communication Breakdown

Well, what I'm not is a rock star and uh, you know, some
people think I am.

—Howard Dean

IN ORDER TO ENERGIZE THE TOWN HALL meetings, rallies, and
fundraisers that stretch a contemporary presidential bid to well over
a year in length, American politicians have become increasingly
reliant on the campaign rock ditty. Nearly all recent races for Chief
Executive have employed rousing soundtracks with lots of power
chords and blunt drumming, all used to motivate their voter bases
in a fist-pumping, Bic-in-the-air sort of way. John Kerry chose Van
Halen's "Right Now." Al Gore opted for Bachman-Turner Overdrive.
George W. Bush played a Tom Petty song for a bit of his reelection
campaign and Michelle Bachmann used Petty's "American Girl"
for a few months, but both quit their songs after Petty threatened
litigation. And poor John McCain was first discouraged from using
an ABBA song, and then outright denied the right to tunes by John
Mellencamp, Boston, Van Halen, Jackson Browne, and Heart before
commissioning a Top 40 country star to write the totally awesome
"Raisin' McCain."

To me, classic rock choices like these say that, along with the increased volume of appearances in a contemporary political bid, there must also be an uptake in aural volume—a post-Baby-Boom expectation of our candidates to take their shtick up to eleven. We expect sonic vigor from someone who promises change. We expect reveille and bombast. We expect jock jams.

And, judging from the vocals in many of these songs, we may also expect a fair amount of yelling. Mellencamp, Sammy Hagar, and Bruce Springsteen (the Boss's songs have been used by at least one candidate in each of the past six elections) are all examples of the vocal style that permeated post-Woodstock rock in the 1970s and '80s—an odd mix of acrobatic crooning and the harsher yells of old blues. Even PBS can explain how such loud and dangerous singing juices us, and how it has done so in bulk for a half-century. We thrill to Springsteen and his laryngeal brethren because their performances wrestle down a product of the body meant to remain unbridled: the uncontrollable scream.

Screamed rock melodies work the outskirts of the voice, bringing an outré sound to an artful place. In classic rock, the ability to hold tight to a beastly scream—to best it despite our biology—is to have unwarranted control over the tones we traditionally reserve for involuntary rage or horrible behavior. This is what made screams the voice of swampy double entendre, of Stagger Lee, of bong hits, of "Wang, Dang, Sweet Poontang." So it is somewhat surprising that we've also allowed rock screams into the dictatorial hype-church surrounding Your Next President.

Let us not forget, too, that the most celebrated rock screams came from bodies that belong to the same subgeneration as our recent front-runners (and their most moneyed supporters). Sammy Hagar was born the same year as Mitt Romney and Hillary Clinton. Rick Perry is seven months older than Tom Petty. Had he attended Cleveland's St. John Cantius High, Bon Scott would have marched with a class of '64 that included Dennis Kucinich. As young men and women, these musicians and politicians must have, in some way, shared a distant context of noisy vocal expression, whether or not they ever scored tickets to a Captain Beefheart show. Like it or not, these men and women are all members of a sort of Screaming Baby Boom.

Plus, in a world of flag pins and $100-a-plate dinners, a hot and ham-fisted rock scream provides a service. The screams of Springsteen, Daltrey, and Scott are aural palate cleansers—blunt sorbets to cut through a two-hour bout of heavy rhetoric. This is because no candidate's words can rile a Carbondale gym like the canned scream of a rock god, especially if the candidate of the hour lacks verbal dynamism (paging Gore, Kerry, Huntsman). Though humans are significantly less attuned to sound than other animals are, we still experience multipronged arousal in the presence of loud noises, especially the noises of our own species. I'm talking about that shot of norepinephrine that drips all over the cerebral cortex, heightening the senses in the presence of a human scream. Elsewhere in the body, it sends a jolt of adrenaline to quicken the heart and tense major muscles, prepping them for a sprint across the veldt away from danger. This hardwiring is what allows dank rock vocalise to connect political agendas with heightened sensory experiences, with socks in the trousers, and, of course, with cool.

What's more, a rock scream that once topped the charts is familiar to us. It might even come off as weirdly trustable to a broad chunk of the voting public. A killer scream from a 70s rock god could sound like a venerable statesman's endorsement of a new and unproven candidate. And in this way, rock screams serve as badass Cyranos: proxy pleas on behalf of the stuffed shirt who skipped Altamont to attend the Alameda County Policeman's Ball. Crank the Stooges in a Muskegon rally, and Iggy himself will tell the crowd that this candidate, along with wanting to exact campaign finance reform, also wants to be our dog.

All these associations, however, must work the crowd subliminally or at least at an absolutely crucial remove. Because no matter how much Hendrix you add to your Town Hall playlist, a candidate and his or her handlers cannot allow a scream to come from the Town Hall stage. Mike Huckabee can play Skynyrd on bass and Bill Clinton can wow Arsenio with his "Heartbreak Hotel" sax skills, but neither man should ever consider opening his mouth to offer a take on the perfect scream in "Won't Get Fooled Again." Those candidates who dare to take their voices into rock-marked territory face a gauntlet of scrutiny. The most memorable example of this is, of course, Howard Dean.

Aside from the scores of classic rock standards piped into its debates and rallies, 2004 was a fairly low-decibel race. Many noted Kerry's Como-like delivery and droning parallel structures, and Edwards' entire shtick was essentially his honey twang, which he kept at a grinning, almost breathy distance from the listener. Al Sharpton was the only true vocalist of the stable of Dems, though his oratory skills snagged fewer and fewer sound bites as his campaign waned. Only two loud moments made big headlines: Democratic Senator Zell Miller's rabid invective at the Republican National Convention and Howard Dean's rant to a thousand of his own "Deaniac" volunteers on the evening of January 19.

Howard Brush Dean III was born in 1948, the exact same year as Vincent Damon Furnier (who would become Alice Cooper), Stephen Victor Tallarico (soon to be Steven Tyler), John Michael (Ozzy) Osbourne, and the greatest of all rock screamers, Robert Anthony Plant. Dean's own multiplatinum recording came in the fifty-sixth year of these five men, long after Plant had defected to bluegrass, Cooper had opened a sports bar, and Osbourne was a reality-TV dad. By 2004, only Tyler still screamed in public, with the help of several corrective surgeries and a nearly operatic level of vocal instruction.

Maybe a Dean scream would have been celebrated had he made it as a younger man, in the style of the rest of the 1948 quintet. Maybe he should have done it shirtless and hopped-up on 'ludes in a Capitol recording studio. Perhaps listeners might have embraced his scream in the Iowa Veterans Memorial Stadium after he bit the head off a bat, like Ozzy did in 1982. In fact, Dean's scream did ring just five miles from Iowa Veterans Memorial, but it came two decades later than Ozzy, in a universe with its own specific sonic laws: the laws of caucus night, the laws of a third-place finish behind Johns Kerry and Edwards, and the laws of netting just eighteen percent of the party vote.

We've all seen the Dean clip, shot from the vantage of the news cameras behind the crowd of West Des Moines' Val Air Ballroom. Shortly after "Baba O'Riley" (in which Roger Daltrey screams "THEY'RE ALL WASTED!") rattles the PA, Dean takes the stage. He crosses past a line of key Iowa campaigners who stand shoulder-to-shoulder: a makeshift backdrop of awkward white people. He shakes hands and hugs a few members of the backdrop, offers one dude a very enthusiastic, very high five. He hands his jacket to Iowa senator Tom Harkin and cuffs his shirtsleeves, and then he takes a deceptively measured breath.

"Wow," he croaks, gently waving his open palm over the audience like a pontiff. "I was about to say I'm sure there's some disappointed people here, but you know something? You know something? If you woulda told us a year ago that we were gonna come in third in Iowa, we woulda given anything for that."

Dean's larynx, like most modern candidates', was surely unaccustomed to the poisons of nonstop campaigning: contaminated motorcades, overheated Sheratons, bitter Iowa air, and exponentially

more hours spent speaking than sleeping. Thus, his tones are notice-
ably belabored in these first sentences. But just as he seems unin-
terested in admitting his unexpected caucus defeat, he also refuses
to accommodate his wounded cords with lowered intensity. There's
a new push in his voice when he continues: "And you know something? You know something?" A crescendo of yells comes from the
crowd.

Here he begins an oft-repeated list of states in the union with
upcoming primaries, rising a bit in pitch and fervor with each one:
"Not only are we going to New Hampshire, Tom Harkin, we're
going to South Carolina and Oklahoma and Arizona and North
Dakota and New Mexico!"

Hundreds of supporters in front of and behind him are yelling
his name, perhaps even screaming a bit. Some people interviewed
after the fact remember yelling "More!" but those prompts are
not audible in the clip. We do hear the stomping of the carpet
and a dozen random cheers. We see various hands, some of them
applauding, some holding glass bottles like torches.

Dean's hands count down the states, first on his right thumb,
then on the whole hand, then with his arms swinging in rhythm
with the names of the final three: "And we're going to California and
Texas and New York, and we're going to South Dakota and Oregon
and Washington and Michigan!"

He playfully tosses the microphone back and forth from hand to
hand. It's a unidirectional mic, meaning its reservoir is designed to
trap his voice and not much else for the clearest possible broadcast.
That mic ignores the crowd and shoots Dean's roll of state names
straight to the cameras in the back. By now, Dean's voice is hard
and low and wet in his throat, a loud growl matched by pointed
brows, bared teeth, and a squint. His use of the simple future tense,
combined with this grimace and rasp, makes Dean seem like a pro
wrestler clad in Brooks Brothers talking ringside smack. What's

more, though the distance from which the clip was filmed makes it difficult to confirm, his diaphragm appears to contract with sharp, forceful breaths after naming each of the last three states. This extra air allows even more juice for his Hulk Hogan tones.

He gulps air once more before the "and" of his final phrase: "And then we're going to Washington, D.C., to take back the White House!" Here is a rise into a question-mark pitch for the last word, then a fist lifted just behind his head. He holds a pose here, like a Maneki Neko Luck Cat, or a slot machine before a pull. Then Dean pauses. But he doesn't inhale. He might even begin an exhale on that pause, stopping the more righteous circle of breath and limiting his respiratory power, which could explain why the final sound of his monologue gets away from him. From there, with his lungs, lips, and larynx in their most politically incorrect positions, Dean makes the sound we care most about, the hostile mutation of a "Yeah!" cheer that many blame for the death of his election hopes.

It is a one-second glissando from an impossibly high note down two full octaves to a flat, guttural trough, as long as a slide down sixteen keys of a baby grand. It is the sound of a Muppet, or a baby in tantrum, or a bike horn half-squeezed. Or, rather, it is all three sounds at different milliseconds, smooshed. It meets his unbuttoned collar and the sloshing bottles and the fibers in that long mic cord and the tone of the Val Air HVAC to make a unique recorded moment—an electric, fantastic, obscene, unspellable thing.

Two-and-a-half years after caucus night, the scream still a rogue part of our lexicon, comedian Dave Chappelle christened it the delicious and onomatopoetic "BYAH!" in a legendary comedy skit. This name has welded itself to the clip and, in some respects, to the man, ever since.

The national broadcast and cable television outlets played the isolated sound over 600 times in the birth week of the "BYAH!"

and the scream's appearances on the radio and Internet were pretty much immeasurable. Drive-time DJ zoo crews, pundit bloggers, and Peter Jennings all played and replayed it, then interviewed experts and voters about it, then played it again. We listeners caught the spreading sound and put it in our pockets or wore it around our necks; we even batted it around a bit ourselves. Tech-savvy self-starters introduced clips of the "BYAH!" that we could program to be the "user error" noise on our cubicle computers. Others had the gumption (and the start-up cash) to embed the scream into novelty gifts, like the Howard Dean Scream the Dream talking bottle opener. A few of us signed up for the Republican Party-sponsored Dean Screaming contest at the 2005 Delaware state fair. We zapped each other jpegs of Dean on the Val Air stage making the scream face, but clutching the neck of a photoshopped kitten in place of the mic. We were creative. We were snide about it. We were not sorry.

Though the website was created sixteen months after Dean withdrew, YouTube is now hundreds of "BYAH!" strong, and these hundreds of videos have collectively accumulated millions of hits and hundreds of thousands of comments. There, nearly a decade after Dean's loud night in West Des Moines, we can access the "BYAH!" both as the mic recorded it and from the more forgiving perspective of an amateur cameraman in the center of the crowd. At that sonic spot, Dean's scream is barely audible among the thousand screaming voices.

A little YouTube window-shopping reveals that we can hear a quarter-speed "BYAH!" forward and backward on a ten-minute loop. We can watch stills of howling moose, fighting zebras, dramatic prairie dogs, and Edvard Munch's screamer with multiple "BYAH!s" as their underscores. We can see a bald infant mime a spot-on "BYAH!" We can learn a club dance to Soulja Boy's "Superman" that mixes Chappelle's 2006 "BYAH!" and Dean's 2004 arm gestures.

We can pit the '04 "Dean Scream" against the '08 "Hillary Cackle." We can hear a "BYAH!" mashed into "Welcome to the Jungle," into Ozzy's "Crazy Train," into "Hey Ya" (renamed, of course, "Hey By-ya!"), and into "Insane in the Membrane."

All these clips teach how Dean's wonky tones, in many respects, have left their parenting body and morphed from language into music—a track too hot to not be dropped. The web illustrates that the "BYAH!"—like the trumpet hook in "Apache" or the bass line in "Boogie Oogie Oogie"—is ripe for sampling.

The b and y of Dean's scream are a flat F in the 5th octave—the same lofty pitch Robert Plant finds at minute 2:09 and 2:11 of "Communication Breakdown." This song, one of Zeppelin's dozen laments to coy mistresses and the blue balls they elicit, features Plant's F during the wordless outro; it is the "WHOA" in his "uh-WHOA-oh!" This is the highest and loudest pitch of the song, and it rises above his established falsetto, above the thrumming rhythm section, above the guitar and the teasing call of the background voices, to ride like a war whoop straight out of the track. Plant's F, as pitch-perfect as any rock scream needs to be, finishes with a drop down to a solid high D, then defiantly repeats—a double backflip of sex and longing that nails its ten-point landing, twice.

In the context of the song, it proves one of two things: either that Plant's character leaves "Communication Breakdown" even more determined to get into the pants of his woman, or that he has actually been driven "insane" by this broken-down communication, and now he's running away, screaming, to go jump off the levee or something. There is a contradiction between Plant's lament—that he can't communicate with the woman he wants—and the two-by-four of bedroom logic bursting from that F-note. That contradiction between the lyric and the sound his body makes is one of the sexiest parts of the song.

Dean's F is wobbly and much less sustained than any of Plant's recorded high notes, and it sounds as if it tickles his false vocal cords, which would make it a more legitimate scream than a part of any sung melody could be. But the "BYAH!" and "Communication Breakdown" Fs are still sonic kin, for a few weird reasons. Both carry a compelling tension within them: these are not the glittery, skywritten Fs of a lyric soprano. The strained energy of these Fs excites and annoys the ear, like how a child's spastic Christmas morning cries buzz the calmer adults around the tree.

What's more, these are not the unplanned yells of men unexpectedly pinned by tractors, or chased by cheetah, or watching the Hindenburg explode. We know Dean and Plant have worked themselves into their particular frenzies, and that both "uh-WHOA-oh!" and "BYAH!" are conscious decisions to dig deep, to go big, and to make highly emotional sounds for a rapt group.

Finally, both bright sounds push away any surrounding noises, assuring that no other tones can blend into them, and this makes the screams stick out in our consciousness. Obviously, microphones emphasize this, but even when mashed up into the alternate Internet landscapes mentioned before, the pitch and timbre of Dean's "BYAH!" stand alone, like a sharp lead vocal in a thrash metal mix. Like so many of Plant's noises, Dean's Val Air F is a lonewolf note that both pops and begs for travel.

These are the elements that made Dick Bennett of the American Research Group note, in the days that followed the "BYAH!", "that thing has legs." Because we can't experience culture-jammed oddities—be they euphonious, silly, or both—just once. We find ourselves reaching out to see if the rest of the world also finds them odd. As with a two-headed calf or third nipple, there is a kind of glee in collecting a leggy note and then revisiting it. That second listen somehow grants us ownership, license to open the curio cabinet again and again, just to see if the pull of the sound is still there—and if it is still just as weird. We laugh selfishly to find out that it remains in our power. And each reappropriated Dean clip that we visit pushes his voice further into our imaginations, light years away from that ballroom, which was the only space in which the "BYAH!" ever had a chance of making sense.

But here is where Dean and Plant differ: one man's sound was added to an arsenal of awesome rock alarums, while the other man's scream became a dangerous metonym for his entire voice, then body, then self. Those 600-plus replays didn't just kill the 2004 Dean campaign; for a little while they erased Dean the man. Though his approval rating was already slipping over the course of caucus week, by the time he left Iowa to head for New Hampshire it had dropped over twenty percent, which many blame on the "BYAH!"

In the week between the scream and the New Hampshire primary, voices from both sides of the aisle marked the sound as a death knell. According to Pat Buchanan, "Dean's Iowa defeat was a real setback to him, but his postgame commentary was a disaster. That tape will be on every national talk show, and I don't think it's survivable." After a tour of several New Hampshire campaign events, Democratic strategist James Carville concurred that "it hurt him," and Leon Panetta explained, "When the country sees that kind of reaction, it makes them nervous because they're looking at a potential president of the *United States.*" Respondents to a poll in *Time* called the "bizarre performance" a chance to hear "the sound of a candidate imploding," while Dick Meyer said that, to many, it unveiled the true voice of Dean as "a hothead, a bully, a chesty, argumentative, inflated, pushy guy you wouldn't want in your poker game." This, says David Bauder of the Associated Press, "turned the former Democratic presidential front-runner into a punch line and arguably hastened his campaign's free fall."

Plant's "uh-WHOA-oh," on the other hand, in no way trumps his coif, his lyrics, or his microphone swing, which are all much more transmutable than the F in question. Dean was outshone because the ethos of an Ivy-League-doctor-turned-governor couldn't keep up with the sound of what Senator Alan Simpson called "a prairie dog on speed." In early 2004, the weaker of the two Deans had to go and, even though the "BYAH!" was nearly four decades younger than both his adult body and his career record, the disembodied sound won by a landslide. Because the "BYAH!" is, like all of Plant's best work, just culturally sluttier.

It's more fun to replay the "BYAH!" than to read Dean's plan to revolutionize healthcare. The sound is easier to think about than his 208-page manifesto on "how to take back the country and restore democracy in America." That army of online "BYAH!" clones serves as an admission that we'd rather access a replicable, goofball bite than the image of an austere politician who says he can fix this country. No Green Mountain politician—even Dean, with his loud online campaign and his rabid bunch of "Deaniacs"—could ever talk over this heavy national impulse. Because, if the past three presidential runs have taught us anything, it's that we can't deny the parts of our ears that like to crank shit up. We listen out for leggy, charged ideas that make us want to stick our heads out of moving cars and shake our hair in the breeze like wet dogs. We'll happily dismiss the idea of a man for a "BYAH!" because "BYAH!" is an open-mouthed jock jam for the soul, one that speaks of things we only half understand. One that makes us run, panting, after it and hollering, as Plant does in the "BYAH!" sister song, "I don't know what it is I like about you but I like it a lot."

This is not to say that the "BYAH!" only spoke to us as a wild meme. Many think that it led listeners to a practical decision: that something about Dean did not compute. Right before the New Hampshire primary, Byron York of the *National Review* said Dean's "red-faced, shouting, teeth-baring, air-punching demeanor" indicated some serious character flaws. A New Hampshire pollster blogger agreed, noting that the scream "kind of crystallize[d] people's fears about Dean—the electability and temperament issues." And after Dean garnered only a quarter of the New Hampshire turnout, David Letterman quipped that voters, in a bit of Sarah Palin reverse-prophecy, "didn't want a president with the personality of a hockey dad."

Both CNN and CBS released statements that admitted to their overplaying the "BYAH!" and even those that did not formally apologize confessed to amping the hype. Their excuse was that the scream was newsworthy; it exposed a hotheaded emotional center that Dean had spent months trying to mask. And that exposure multiplied because, to quote an ABC News senior vice president, "the amount of attention it was receiving necessitated more attention." They then cited Dean's earlier trail gaffes and smatterings of colorful language as just cause. We were informed that All of America—all of us—was nervous. We sensed what a few writers called Dean's hidden "mad How" disease, his secret short fuse. The TV buzz told us that the yell contradicted what a candidate's persona should be, and insisted that we were shocked to see such a display of unbridled anger.

But perhaps we should give our ears more credit than they did.

For starters, voters don't necessarily consider fired-up noises to be non-presidential. A 2007 CBS News poll found that 57 percent of Americans would elect a president with a reputed temper. Political journalist John Dickerson notes that Nixon, Johnson, and Kennedy's White House tapes are all full of ranting and profanities, which historians treasure in hindsight, even though few invectives were ever within earshot of the nation. What's more, in 2010, reporters and commentators balked at Obama's even-toned response to the BP oil spill, saying the president wasn't acting angry *enough* to satisfy the American people. So, apparently, the commanders of our armed forces are all but expected to have a war cry within them. Maybe not a fifth-octave F war cry, but some loud, angry noise.

Dickerson adds that presidents are allowed to erupt in public *before* they take office, especially at the beginning of primary season. This was the case with Reagan's 1980 outburst in New Hampshire ("I AM PAYING FOR THIS MICROPHONE, MISTER GREEN") and Clinton's heated 1992 speech in a New York supper club ("I have treated you and all of the other people who have interrupted my rallies with a hell of a lot more respect than you have treated me, and it's time you started thinking about THAT!"). Both these yells garnered applause from their audiences and spurred only misdemeanor backlashes.

Further, though we never got the chance to see him hide his rage in office, John McCain ran *two entire campaigns* on a loud and angry line. The 2000 and 2008 McCains were slow-burn brutes whose frustration with Washington's bullshit were jackhammered into his furrowed brow. McCain went on *Saturday Night Live* and parodied his trademark anger in skits about Barbra Streisand and Tim Russert, to the delight of the late-night audience. So, if the "BYAH!" told us Dean was angry about his surprise loss in Iowa, or that his fight back to first place would be fueled by rage, there is precedent that this should not bother us. History suggests Dean wouldn't be completely counted out just for sounding fierce.

Seventy-two hours after the scream, Diane Sawyer asked Judy Dean if she had ever witnessed "BYAH!" level rage in her married life. She said no, dismissing her husband's "BYAH!" as a "silly" noise he just happened to emit, as if it were a fart at a dinner party. Then Dean, who sat at her side, said his sound came not from rage, but from concern for his young Deaniacs: "It was really tough for those kids who worked their hearts out and [to then] come in third when they thought I was going to come in first. You know? I'm a little sheepish,

Diane, but I'm not apologetic because I was giving everything to people who gave everything to me."

"Worked their hearts out" is beautifully figurative, rebranding passionate grassroots campaigning as some sort of ultimate physical gift. It links the exhausted Deaniacs to Pheidippides the messenger after his long run down the Marathon road, or to Janis Joplin's "waaughyaaugh, take it!"—that perfect, flattened howl in which she actually tries to sing "a little piece of my heart" out of her body. Was Dean's scream, then, trying to work his body à la Joplin, squatting low enough into his throat to heave several of his vital organs out with the sound? Is this the "everything" he was trying to "give" back to those kids?

If so, then the "BYAH!" once again shouldn't have turned us off at all. In film, in sports, in religion, and in rock, we live for such wholehearted presents from Lance Armstrong, from Al Pacino, from James Brown, from Jesus. Further, how is the scream of a candidate shaking loose his heart to soothe his constituents *not* politically admirable? Don't voters revel in the idea of a leader who cares about America to the point of self-harm? And how is a campaign "waaughyaaugh, take it!" not the antithesis of Washington fat-cattery?

But let us not forget Dean took that stage in West Des Moines to give a small concession. He was up there to admit that yes, a week before, he was slated for an easy caucus win, and yes, for over six months he had been the front-runner for the Democratic party, but now he was in third place. Yes, the day before he made a few stops in Iowa to venues in which the campaign staff outnumbered the constituents. And sure, twenty-four hours before the Val Air Ballroom, writer Walter Shapiro had already compared him to "an aging rock star reduced to reprising his greatest hits in smaller and smaller clubs." And he had to admit that he'd spent at least $45 million, nearly half of which came from tiny online pledges, to get to these Iowa clubs. And yes, a half-million people had rallied behind this man with no national political experience, 3,500 of them quitting their jobs or leaving school to knock on doors in key caucus cities. And he had to own up to the fact that his gaffes, paired with his antiwar, repeal-the-tax-cuts stances, trumped all that human sweat. Collectively, they made him appear so easy to defeat that the *National Review* put his face on their cover with the headline "Please Nominate This Man."

He was too vulnerable, and as he rolled up his sleeves and hugged Tom Harkin, maybe that fact was finally heavy in his gut, lungs, and throat. Maybe that scream was part of the acknowledgment that even Dean had seen the buttons—"dated Dean, married Kerry"—in Des Moines, Mason City, Ottumwa, and Cedar Falls. Dean himself told Diane Sawyer, "I say things that I probably ought not to say, but I lead with my heart, and that's what I was doing right there, leading with my heart." Maybe this little piece of his heart jumped into his lungs, past the trachea and out the bared slot of his mouth, only to contradict the rally cry he'd spoken immediately before it. This, I think, is what we heard.

This is not to say that we heard the contradiction between his triumphant monologue and the conciliatory "BYAH!" and then voted him out for being dishonest. America understands that a president can't always tell the whole truth, and studies show that, as long as they aren't lying about voluptuous interns or campaign spies, we're cool with it. According to a 2010 CNN poll, 74 percent of Americans think George Washington probably lied to his constituency, and over two-thirds of the country think even Lincoln lied (albeit for the good of his country's citizens). Besides, what good coach wouldn't be forgiven an exaggerated speech, maybe even a little "Eye of the Tiger," after losing the first game of a big season?

I think what we heard in the sound is that it was over, that Dean's body had admitted defeat before his brain did. The "BYAH!" let us know that that was it, and we should now just go home and get on our computers or something. Dean's will or reason could fight it, but the parts of him that made the "BYAH!" are louder than will or reason, and older than microphones, or *Hardball*, or oxford shirts, or healthcare, or even Tom Harkin. They are older than speech. They are at least as old as the practice of yelling to a drum beat.

On January 19, we heard Dean's body tell us that we were not going to go to California or Connecticut or Georgia or Maryland or Massachusetts or Ohio or Rhode Island or Minnesota, or to Washington, D.C., to take back the White House. Instead, we heard that we were going to board a plane to Portsmouth and land in a frozen hangar filled with 500 Yankee Deaniacs who were just like us. Someone was going to find the perfect jock jam for that New Hampshire predawn—it ended up being Tom Petty's "I Won't Back Down"—but the 56-year-old body that took the stage, grooving a little to Tom Petty's measured, middle-aged baritone, was not going to scream out of the track like a rock star.

We could hear that, in four weeks—before Super Tuesday, even—we would see him stop moving. And that two months from now, he would endorse John Kerry, then campaign to chair the Democratic National Committee. And that in seven years, he would still be on our televisions, but we would only be able to see his head and shoulders, his wild arms and body cut out of the frame like Elvis's were on *Sullivan*. His tie would be knotted and he would glare at us head on, surrounded by tweets and text boxes and stock tickers. He would have joined the machine that shamed him, now talking politics and YouTube clips on a cable news show. And that the show would be called, fittingly, *Squawk Box*.

The Zealot

I remembered what the woman had said about the tongue, and I praised hard, yearning for my tongue to be taken. Then it was, and it began to move like a trip-hammer. I began to use sounds and syllables that I did not recognize. Behold, I was speaking in tongues. My tongue was moving faster than I could ever move it in normal conversation, and I was not in the least tired, nor were my hands tired as they had been earlier in the evening, though they shook and shook. My whole body was refreshed.

I spoke in tongues; then I sang in tongues, the syllables seeming to match the music; then I prayed in tongues. I was in burden and squirmed on the floor. All at once I was seized with "holy weeping," and I wept until I thought my heart would break. Then suddenly I was seized with "holy laughter"; I was under the grip of this power. I behaved as one hysterical, and yet I had never had hysterics in all my life.

After some time had elapsed, this power released me, and I began to quiet down. I opened my eyes and looked around. It was close to midnight. I stood to walk but was so dizzy from the experience that I had to reach for the back of a pew to steady myself from falling. Think of it—dizzy from lying on a floor. . . . As I steadied myself, the Scripture came to my mind, "Others mocking said, These men are full of new wine."

———

So I let out a shout, for I was thereby assured that I had the true baptism of the Holy Ghost.

Harpy

HERE IS ALL I CAN TELL YOU ABOUT WHAT it sounds like when I open my mouth and scream.

My scream moves through a body that has been in working order for over thirty-three years. It is a five-foot-six-and-one-half-inch female body, around 140 pounds, and its bone structure appears larger than those of most women I see in the park or at the gym or in the market. Only one of these larger-than-average bones—a metatarsal—has broken, but this still affects the body posture and thus, according to some, the resonance of the voice. I think, however, that the warped state of the neck and shoulders after years in front of a laptop alters the sound much more significantly. Twenty-five and a half percent of this body is fat and up to sixty percent of it is water. It is not without its tonsils or its appendix and it has never been impregnated. All these things are a part of the sound you hear when I sigh, sing, or say "hello," or scream it.

My lower ribcage circumference measures thirty-five inches after a very deep inhale, and thirty-one and a half inches after I've expelled all possible air from my lungs. I can hold my breath for as long as it took me to type the last sentence three times in a row, including a few pauses to correct typos. My neck is thirteen inches around.

My vocal tract and its surrounding pipes are probably thirty centimeters long. The cords that produce speech and sound are approximately fifteen millimeters in length. They were white when I was born, but in the past fifteen years I have tinted them with lots of coffee, more than a little alcohol, scores of nights in smoky places and a few hundred cigarettes. I spent eighteen years in a house with heavy indoor smokers. I then spent nine years in a city with a high level of pollution. The remaining six years of my life, I have breathed relatively cleaner air, and I've yet to acquire either asthma or respiratory allergies, which would add new timbre to the resonance of the cells in the body.

•

For most of my twenties, I used my voice to make money, as an actor in plays that required lots of talking, some singing, and the occasional scream. When I wasn't getting regular performance work, I read radio copy into microphones, or hollered to be heard over bunches of kids in elementary school theaters. Back then, my voice was strong and easy to command. I lost it only once, when I was double-booked, rehearsing a sex farce in the afternoons and evenings while performing a one-woman show about Rachel Carson every morning. When my voice began to wane, the sex farce director ordered me to mime all my communications outside of rehearsal, to never whisper, to eat apples, to avoid clearing my throat, and to drink tepid water "till your pee is clear." This worked.

The last time I screamed for money was four years ago, when a repertory theater in Iowa hired me to give an extended Hammer Horror scream for a zany comedy about Niagara Falls. This was a loud, high scream for which I did a very silly ten-minute vocal warm-up and watched clips of Jamie Lee Curtis in *Halloween*. Curtis is a wonderful screamer. Both in 1978 and in the *Halloween* remake twenty years later, she leaps from her tawny alto into a bright, steely cry. She's girlier in screams than she is in speech, really.

That mock-Curtis scream was the last one I remember attempting, either impromptu or for hire, and when I remember it now, I don't hear the sound of the scream. Instead, I picture the red-silhouetted gobo onto which I fixed my gaze. I feel myself inhale and remember the fear that the sound about to leave my mouth wouldn't be the sound I planned. Then I feel the scream rattle before it begins. The actual sound of the scream, however, is lost. I do know that it wasn't nearly as easy as the screams I made in my early life, when such sounds were more frequent and more fun.

•

On the first day of spring in 1978, my mother lay on a papered medical table, her feet still in her espadrilles. She was on her way to the beach a few hours earlier, but, according to her, I insisted she take a detour. After a long hour of lying there, she screamed bloody murder into the doctor's ear.

"What in God's name did you do that for?" the doctor asked.

"That's how they sound on television," she answered.

"Don't do it again," he said.

According to my mother, I was born screaming, like every other healthy baby. I wonder if she actually recalls these first screams, or if, like the sounds of her labor, she's aligned this experience with blessed celluloid events. And what did it feel like to push such a loud thing out of herself? This weighted, crucial thing that she no doubt imagined meeting for months, which promptly shot a hello at her in the form of the biggest, most evil noise it was capable of making. And I wonder what it was like to scream without teeth, without neck muscles, without the ability to ground the vibrations in my planted legs and feet. Mom says I spent the first several hundred nights of my life screaming the paint off the thin walls of the apartment we shared, quieting only when she sang a lullaby about a slaughter-bound calf who wished he were a bird. While I doubt that a song like that would calm anyone, I do trust that these screams existed, building the tissue in my throat, stretching my lungs and my belly. Because I know how the voice box tenses and relaxes to meet air in my adult body. I know the sensation of bracing myself for high volume. Even when I hum under my breath, I can sense those crucial false flaps hanging, unused and mutant, beside the mechanism that helps me swallow.

·

I think it is also important to tell you that my mother is one of the loudest people I have known in my life. I'm not speaking figuratively when I tell you that her voice shook the foundations of the houses we shared. When I was teenaged and would appear sullen and unladylike in public, she would lecture me, and I would snap back at her, "Gah, stop yelling at me." She'd correct my semantics, first in her speaking voice: "I don't think I've raised my voice to you, young lady. This is not yelling." And then with ten times the power—"THIS! IS! YELLING!"—at a decibel level rarely heard in our suburb's grocery stores and shopping malls.

She could stand on the back porch and call me home from any yard in the subdivision; I loved trying to yell back at a matching volume. When she had dinner parties and I was sent upstairs to bed at ten, I could never sleep, never even lie still, thanks to the heavy scaffold of her party voice, which wound through the joists that separated the two floors of our house and then yanked me out of my bed.

There was a photo book in our stereo cabinet of her years in a college drama club, which included a turn as Abigail, the manipulative teenage instigator of *The Crucible*. Abigail derails the big witch trial in Act Three by screaming at an imaginary demon bird that she says hovers above her in the courthouse rafters. Mom liked to tell the story of how her classmates jumped at her scream, how it rang in the air like some new drug. And I liked imagining her—bonnet, pinafore, long false eyelashes—pointing upward and opening her mouth. I could see the audience's necks jerking from the center to downstage right to follow the force of this dark girl and her huge sound, which had cut a yellow gash in the air.

•

Miller's script says Abigail "screams up to the ceiling," ordering the actress to give a "weird, chilling cry" that marks the courtroom's (and the trial's) descent into madness. It is fun to believe that a young girl's voice can "chill" a room, like a fan blown over a block of ice. The "chill" of it is, I think, the lofted pitch of the female scream, the sound of our species' smallest vocal tracts jumping into the grip of their necks and held away in a pitch too high for speech. For this reason, it makes sense to score females as the instruments of dramatic fear in film and theater. Also, women's screams are the highest full-voice notes on the market, as our boxes are generally the shortest and least hormonally bolstered. Because they are lighter, they can fly.

It is this icy, upper register chill that made "scream queens" like Jamie Lee Curtis, Fay Wray, and my favorite screamer, Adrienne Barbeau, famous—well, that and how juicily they filled out their costumes. Wray's screams are random and perfect, peppered all over *King Kong*, and she launches them into the skyline, as sonically impossible as the high Cs of the lead tenor in *La Fille du Régiment*. I love the little points at the end of her dozen poison-dart screams, as if she were dancing over her giant ape in a pair of stilettos.

In *The Fog* and the *Halloween* films, Jamie Lee Curtis's screams serve as sonic buttons at the ends of long builds. Mind you, these are builds that depend on scoring and editing as much as the work of the actress. One need look no further than Curtis's mother, Janet Leigh, to see proof of this, as her muscular scream is lower in pitch, and thus crushed by the classic violins in Bernard Herrmann's stab-theme to *Psycho*.

But something about this instrumental relationship between screamer and scene has always made ladylike scream queens sound fabricated to me, like Abigail's bird in the Salem courthouse. The soprano scream of fear, while musical and gorgeous, rings as rehearsed, or at least conditioned: a biological response that has been culturally taught, like those of us who sneeze both syllables in "ah-choo."

•

I tried to mimic what I imagined to be my mother's Abigail scream when I was a girl, in my high school's production of *The Crucible*, but I might have overdone it. My Abigail had flatter hair and wore bigger slippers than my mother's, but I too thrilled in the silence right before my own scream, in the way my ears woke up on the deep inhale. Internally, it felt like a purring motor in my body. My lungs felt pink and huge and invincible.

Whatever it sounded like, I lobbed it up into the auditorium like a granny-shot cannonball. Mothers jumped and kids giggled. I heard my English teacher yelp, "Oh, for Pete's sake." My friend Tommy, who drew cartoons for the school newspaper, later gave me his copy of the program, on which he had doodled a long-haired bubble-head in a Puritan costume, with black squiggles for eyebrows and a pointy, hinged mouth like a fox trap. A shocked audience sat below the hairy bubblehead, and above her were three figures in a light booth with their hands over their headphoned ears.

•

The only time I recall screaming from actual fear was when, at fifteen, I got myself lost in the Florida woods. Enamored by the palm trees and nature trails, I forgot that I had never been camping, never been a Girl Scout, let alone some kind of off-trail hiker, and I traipsed way too far into the Gulf Coast brush, where all the marked trees look the same. After about three hours of circling the same square mile, an armadillo ran just in front of my flip-flopped foot and I sank to the dirt path, gasping.

I thought about my mother, how she would find me here in my frayed khaki shorts and the ringer tee I bought for a quarter at the thrift store. She would scissor the clothes from my ruined corpse, then find a pastel twin-set to dress me in for the funeral. She would ask the mortician to wax my eyebrows. I thought of the time I was a flower girl in a hot church in Charleston and I passed out at the altar. My buddy the ring bearer said my mother screamed, right there in front of God and everybody, when she saw me tip over. I thought of that horrible song about the bird and the slaughter-bound calf, and then—perhaps because this is what they do in the movies—I started screaming out in the middle of nowhere.

I screamed the word "no" and then I screamed the word "somebody." I only murmured the word "please." And the word I screamed the longest was the word I wasn't allowed to use after age four or five, "Mommy," and I screamed it full voice for what felt like thirty minutes. I don't remember listening to myself, but I still feel the way it came with fluidity from a very wrong physical place, as if I had a new mouth in my stomach. After a while, it felt worse to stop screaming, so I forced myself to continue, as if the sound of my voice were a solution. My body had decided that once it stopped screaming, it had nothing.

•

I have never heard my mother make the sound of the high scream queens, though I got to know the sounds of her fear and her anger very well. I assume most close-quartered groups get this sonic education, especially children, who, by their adolescence, can categorize the sounds of the adult voices in their lives: the innocuous tones of a squabble; the tense, punchy sounds of an hour of bickering; the scary, ignitable pitches of a voice doused with cocktails. One tone that rarely buzzed our walls spoke of a particularly terrifying outrage, and I grew able to hear it flip in my mother's voice like a switch.

It was less silvery than the scream queens', lower in her gut, with a beefy fuzz, like a gauge straining into the red. It sounded as if it could push furniture. I heard it once when she tried to pull the television off its stand and throw it out a second-story window; once again when she was chasing my stepfather down the stairs and into the basement. Listening to it while lying still in bed was a very lonely torture; I felt tiny, even when I was teenaged and already outweighed her. In the foreign airspace that was two or three or four in the morning, I would feel the urge to lace my hands behind my neck and get under a desk.

But I also felt compelled to move *closer*, to see the way her body changed when she switched from her brassy mezzo trumpet to this blistering and reptilian sound. Every note of it sounded damaging: to her insides, to the air of our house. I remember picturing a werewolf holding his hand before his face and watching the claws burst away from his knuckles.

•

Years later, I heard the Pixies' "Tame," with Frank Black's deep-tissue, one-word screams at minute 1:43, and I thought, *Ahhhh, yes.* And once again when I read *A Streetcar Named Desire*, in which Williams scripts Stanley Kowalski to scream "STELL-LAHHHHHH!" with what his stage directions call "heaven-splitting violence."

•

For the past three years, I've used my voice less and less. I don't do theater in this town, and I avoid long phone conversations or chatty nights in bars. My boyfriend works very late on weekends and then sleeps until lunchtime, so my days off can pass without speaking more than a few lines of baby talk to my cats. On the street in front of the window where I type this, people scream "That's not my motherfucking problem!" into small phones, held out a few inches away from their mouths. Mothers engage in full-voice monologues to babies about rules and backtalk, and couples howl at each other on the street. On the bus yesterday, four undergrads screeched with laughter in some kind of deafening storytelling contest about vomit. The rest of us bent our cell phones closer to our torsos and text messaged.

In this new era of personal quiet, sometimes I can actually feel my voice shrinking. Songs I love will come on in the car, but I don't like the sounds I make when I sing along to them. At the end of my longer days of teaching, my voice is clenched, thirsty, and dull. Right now, just thinking about screaming on stage or in a karaoke bar makes my stomach lurch a bit. The only place I might feel wholly comfortable to scream would be at the top hill of a roller coaster, or just outside a plane after I've jumped from it. I screamed a little at a GWAR show last year, just because I was sure nobody around me was listening. And even then, among those distracted man-boys covered in slime and cornstarch, I was still self-conscious about overdoing it.

•

I suppose all this led to my entering the 2011 Stella Shouting Contest, which was held one hundred years and one day after Williams' birth as a part of the Tennessee Williams Literary Festival. For twenty-five years, contestants have stood under a wrought-iron balcony in New Orleans and screamed "Stella!" up to an actress in a slip (for women bold enough to enter, they put a Brandoish Stanley actor up there, too). The five best screamers then advance to an indoor theater a block away, where a group of celebrity judges decide who yelled "Stella!" best—except in 2006, when the winner they selected had opted to scream "FEMA!" instead.

The prize is a trophy and gift certificates for things like river dinner cruises and rock'n'bowling, but the real reward for me was a sanctioned, command-performance scream, a situation in which nothing *less* than a scream would be expected. And along with this license came the rare opportunity to embody a great American vocal moment in some kind of iconic karaoke. To stand on a cobblestone street, funky with sweat and booze, and think of Kowalski, and then holler in the actual shadow of Brando's unkillable sound. I decided I would train like Rocky, fly to New Orleans, and chart my screams when they came from my mouth in a way that would allow me to finally remember them.

I conned my friend Paul—a Brit who loves Brando almost as much as he does strange American rituals—into flying to New Orleans, hoping he'd keep me from chickening out on the day. That morning, as we walked around the Garden District, I told him I was worried that I couldn't control the sound that came out of my mouth, not that it would be unladylike or frowzy, but that it would be a dead boring sound. I had been practicing "Stella!" on my drives home from work, and when I listened to myself in the car, my voice didn't seem like it would make it up to a second-floor balcony. Plus, the noise I made, while decidedly ugly, also sounded so uninspired, like no heavens would ever split from its wimpy magnitude. I asked what he thought "heaven-splitting violence" sounded like.

"Low," he said, "more passionate. I think you would do better dredging up some dark emotion."

I told him that, with my life, my cats, and my books and my patient boyfriend, my unbroken bones, my good job and the quiet of my comfortable apartment, I was beginning to worry that I didn't have much to dredge.

"Oh, come off it," he replied. "Who doesn't?"

•

I had been watching YouTube clips of Shout Out screamers. They stood in Jackson Square with their backs to the Mississippi and let it rip for Stella and hundreds of onlookers. The final rounds were full of clever gimmicks—a mime mouthing his three "*Stella!*s," a Saints fan screaming "Who Dat, Stella," a tiny child in a Brando tee and slicked-back hair. All but two of the clips I found were of men; a man had won every year since the contest began in the 1980s. The only woman I saw who even made it to the finals offered a screech that was anything but powerful, but she also ripped off her tank top at the end of her third "Stella!," revealing a lack of brassiere.

There is one YouTube clip of a fair-haired man whimpering between each fraught "Stella!" and I liked him best of all. His hands flutter around him, making him look smaller and more crippled by Stanley's tragic shame. And his final "Stella!" is quite long, so that the guttural growl in the *e*-sound has time to build into the *a*-sound, and then taper back out again. It also doesn't hurt that his torso looks the most like Brando's in a thin white tee.

The man is Matt Payne, a chipper New Orleans assistant district attorney who first entered the contest in 2002, when he ranked in the finals. I asked Payne what led him to make that noise out in front of a mass of strangers. "I did it because it's a ridiculous way to spend an afternoon," he said, "but also because it's an acceptable release. You're letting it all out, everything you've been through, and you feel everyone wishing they could do what you do—just get down on your knees and scream your ass off."

Payne won the grand prize the second time he entered, in 2009, after deciding to give the judges "the full Irish," (which was difficult, he says, "because I'm only half Irish"). For Payne, "full Irish" means the ability to bring his adult body to an infantile state of distress. When he was standing under Stella's balcony the second time, Payne thought about when he was little, living with his mother and four siblings while his Dad was on naval deployment. His mighty temper tantrums were so terrifying that his mother would record them, then threaten to mail the cassettes to Payne's father if he didn't behave. Channeling that tape-tantrum worked for the Shout Out, he says, because Brando's Stanley is "just a big baby, really. He can't see the future, he can't figure anything out."

•

Professor Sheila McKenna, an actor and the Chair of Theatre at Point Park University's Conservatory of Performing Arts, sees the "Stella!" scream as a kind of raw and inarticulate apology. "I don't think he actually says 'I'm sorry' anywhere in that scene, does he? Even after all the shit he pulled," she says. "He can't do it; he ain't gonna do it—he might not even know how. But he knows he has to make a sound."

Getting to that sound, she says, involves using the whole body to contribute to the scream. In her voice classes, actors lie on the floor and hum, feeling their breath not just in their chests and throats, but in their calves, upper arms, backs, and skulls. They aren't training their bodies to do something new, however; they are remembering speech as the full-body event it once was. According to her, Matt Payne isn't far off with his tantrum connection, since babies can scream for hours at a time and never hurt themselves. "That's because they use their whole bodies to cry," she says. "They aren't listening to their voices; the voice is a part of a body that is using all of itself to get what it wants."

McKenna says she'd coach a Stanley by first asking him to consider the "physical circumstances" of that moment under the balcony: how Stanley's body holds itself in drunkenness, in stunted arousal, in the face of impending fatherhood, in the aftermath of a blue-collar workday. Once he felt his body reacting to all these "pressors" ("not pressures, but pressors," she stresses), the sound would come from the breath working inside these emotional places.

One day when we were discussing my bid for Shout Out champion, I told McKenna I was interested in solidifying a golden noise that was both real and impressive, a tight aria that wove the fear of a scream-queen scream with the rage of a Stanley Kowalski scream. I wanted it to be something I could cultivate and count on, a sound guaranteed to make the audience want to duck under the statue of Andrew Jackson and hide. McKenna chided me. "You can't think about one sound as a thing to shoot for or replicate," she said. "Those kinds of sounds are just museum theater."

•

At around 3:30 in the afternoon, Paul and I joined the clump of contestants clogging the pedestrian traffic in Jackson Square. The registrar asked how to spell my last name twice, then asked how to pronounce it, and finally just gave me a huge card marked number eleven. "Now go take some time to practice your best 'Stanleee!'" he said, then winked. The guy in line behind me had placed fourth in the 2010 Shout Out, and was convinced that this was his year. I asked him for advice. He stared me down like a football coach. "What you need to do right now? Is get away from this crowd. You need to go somewhere else and get into the zone, and get yourself ready." I decided against asking him where "the zone" was.

Over half of the first-round contestants were jocular guys. Most of them wore white undershirts, and a lot of them were already yelling at each other in the registration line. One middle-aged guy with a forceful Eastern Seaboard accent kept hollering "ALLRIGHT BABY!" with the natural resonance of all men who, for years, have played the Fun Loud Guy at parties, at work, at church. A news crew interviewed the East Coast guy before he even went on. There were also performer types in the line—a gold-painted street statue, a mustachioed ringmaster whose spooky, taciturn lady friend held his top hat, and several shiny men with good posture and bright, darting eyes that I quickly recognized as actors.

The only other woman I saw in line was a thin punk with sleeves of tattoos, a fedora, and a fake mustache. A little plastic gun was shoved into the waistline of her pants. She made me want my own camouflage and props; I felt like an idiot for coming armed with nothing save some ideas about vocal placement and a thin gray Lady Hanes tank top I'd wadded into my purse. Paul stood guard while I changed shirts in an alley behind an oyster bar, then we paced the neighboring blocks of the square while I drank three bottles of water.

By then, a huge crowd had horded around an empty patch of the street in a sort of unkempt Soul Train line. One obviously inebriated man in a straw hat was complaining that the Stanley they'd perched on the balcony was too pretty (it was actually 2009 champ Matt Payne up there). The drunk man pointed me to a bearded heavyweight drinking a wine cooler a few balconies over. "Now THAT's a Stanley," he said. He eyeballed me after I told him I was a contestant, and that I planned to yell not to Matt/Stanley, but to the pretty Stella in a black slip that was up there next to him.

"Now that just doesn't make sense," he said.

"Why not?"

"Because Stanley was a man and Stella is a woman. The man shouts at the woman."

"But what does the woman get to do?"

"She's the one stands up there and is yelled to; that's what it's about. And she, you know, gets beat."

•

There's another Abigail stage direction in *The Crucible*, one that calls for a silent implosion rather than a scream. It comes in a scene Miller cut from the play, but that many directors still include, because it is so electric. Shortly before the witch trial, the play's protagonist, bold and principled John Proctor, meets young Abigail in the woods late at night. Instead of responding to her advances the way he once did, he catches her in a criminal lie. Here, despite her persuasiveness and her longing, despite how frequently her bad behavior is forgiven in Salem, Abigail will not get her way.

"A wildness stirs in her," Miller instructs. "A child is standing here who is unutterably frustrated, denied her wish, but still she is grasping for her wits." Miller calls it "unutterable," but I don't see much of a difference between Abigail's infantile frustration and Stanley's bratty vocabulary, up to and including "STELL-LAHHHHHH!"

Both characters are more bossy and charismatic than they are smart; both seem capable of a frightening brutality. At the moments in question, both are in trouble, shamed and denied the attention of their lovers. But Stanley is given a vocal demand to push his warped agenda; he gets to use his voice to call for what he wants. Abigail's frustration, however, cannot be uttered. She must feel her frustration, then swallow it.

•

Each contestant got to yell three times, and I have no idea if the judges were scoring the composite of the three, or the best scream. I have a feeling their process was not all that regulated. Ten screamers went ahead of me, and I counted them down like steps to the end of a gang-plank. The East Coast guy's "Stella!" was a wonderful twin of Lou Costello's "Hey Ab-BOTT!" A fratty dude tossed out "Stella!" from the middle of his mouth, like Dean Martin in "Volare." A wiry guy in a black singlet zoomed through all three "*Stella!*s," then ran away. Shortly before my turn, someone finally called for Stanley—a gray-haired woman in a patio dress that appeared to be made of hemp. She did not scream at all. Her voice was drippy and low, with that throaty burble that comes when you're trying to stifle tears. She swayed like a torch singer as she called for him, grabbing her long skirt, show-ing leg. She even ad-libbed a little: "I *need* you, baby! I *need* my *man!*"

Matt Payne-as-Stanley hollered back, "I'll be right down!'"

When they called for number eleven, I promptly forgot anything anyone had told me, anything I had planned to do or to say or to avoid. My perspective shifted into that warped lens of performance in which my body decides things without processing them. Commands happened inside me like lines in a Beckett one-act: Hands hold number eleven entry card; hands throw card. Open hands; stretch hands wide. Eyes move upward; eyes stare. Hands point; eyes glower. Hands are trembling; hands make fists. Knees bend, lungs billow, neck twists, voice screams.

•

The Shout Out crowd was close enough to mess with my periphery. I thought if I raised my hands too wide I would slap them, but when I saw clips of the scream later, I noticed they were several feet away. Still, when your listeners are so near and so large in number, you can sense how loud your own sounds are without actually hearing them.

The feel of them listening bounces back to you, reports whether the scream is wild enough and loud enough, and if you are being called upon to do it again, or if you will merely be tolerated until you finish. If you will be accepted, despite your breasts, while yelling a lady's name. If so, then the shoulders push back; the chest pushes forward. Buckle knees; swing arms. Touch dirty ground with fingers, palms. Roll backward; constrict thighs, pull body forward. Rend garment. Belly lifts, voice screams.

•

My mother is now almost sixty, and she lives alone for the first time in her life. Even though science says menopause should have winnowed the mucus that oils her larynx, she has still got quite a voice. The last time I saw her, she was cleaning out her refrigerator, yanking the empty shelves from their perches to rinse them in the sink. As a few dislodged, they slipped out of her wet fingers. She struggled to catch them, and the sound she made as they fell was so loud that her china rattled in its cabinet. It was, of course, the loudest voice I'd heard in weeks.

I knew from our Sunday phone conversations that, ever since my mother's second marriage dissolved, she had been piling all the fallout into herself. But watching her yell at the fridge shelves like that was jarring enough to stick inside me. As a child, I saw something mighty in her tiny frame when it attacked household chores at high volume; now I always feel troubled, because every sound she makes—even laughter—reeks of a deep and almost resigned soreness. It is impossible for a listener to escape the fact that massive crises reshape the column of a throat, the muscles of a back, the body that must force itself upright until sundown, when it pours at least two cocktails for itself and then passes out and yells in its sleep.

•

The finals were held indoors, in a little theater on St. Peter Street. There were five contestants waiting backstage: myself, the veteran screamer who had coached me in line, the patio-dress wailer, the tattooed chick with the gun in her pants, and a distractingly brawny LSU student with the eyes of an eager puppy. A majority of women finalists for the first time ever, a festival administrator told me. We all paced and waited. Someone spread a rumor that there would be cake afterward.

It might just have been the hard liquor I had mainlined between the preliminaries and finals, but something changed once I noticed that I could smell the stage floor, with its decades of coats of paint, as well as the dank walls and dusty curtain fabric. In small, very old theaters like these, even the lights have a smell. They were such familiar odors that they comforted me. I knew that, in the weird autopilot that is my onstage brain, I could use them to map the theater's acoustics. I could shoot sound toward not just the expectant judges, but the layers of paint and the musty lights. My body relaxed; it was ready to yell in a room like this. And then they called my name, I was the second screamer of our bunch, and I stopped paying attention.

•

A woman up in the balcony made an iPhone movie that began when I walked onstage, and she posted it as "Yay! A girl is the winner of the Stella Shouting Contest in New Orleans!" So now I can tell you more about what happens when I scream. In her video, I am just a faraway outline of myself, waving limbs and a washed-out head and, when I turn sideways, a little pot belly. My hands are always tense, either fists or claws. In between the first and second screams,

I gasp, and I just keep breathing in, trying to extend the last vowel of "Stella!" through the inhale. The crowd howls at this. After the second "Stella!," I shake my head vigorously, like the scream is a whiskey shot that burns as I swallow it. I have no idea where any of these ideas came from.

The third scream, I think, is the scream that won it. You can hear me lose a battle in my throat. You do not have to assume that I will be mute for days afterward; you know it. Because on the *e* of that last "Stella!," the sound sinks lower into my neck and starts ripping. Imagine the margin of a piece of paper torn, notch by notch, from a spiral notebook, or an anvil dropping through floor after floor of a cartoon tenement. I did not tell myself to make this hurt, but there I am, punching lower and lower into myself to see what comes up. The noise is just awful, but it is mighty loud.

•

In that scaly, winning sound, I think, is the last thing I can tell you about my body when it screams. I can say that inside of me—and in you too, probably—is first a place in which muscle and air stop being useful, where our body tells us sound is no longer possible. This is on the corporeal map that we use every day, even at our louder moments—even, perhaps, on stage.

But I now know that when I rile myself up to the point of damage and think hard about the sounds that scare me most, I can rummage around inside for a second bottom to that map-able place, and I can mine *that* for sound. It's a sad discovery, I suppose, this lonely and untapped sonic pocket with a trap release, but I do not know what is sadder about it: that it lies there, useless, sometimes for an entire quiet life, or that something allows me to trick myself into finding it. Or that it exists in us at all.

Because this means that a space inside all of us waits for something that hurts so much that we require it. It is built not for fear or for flight, but for need. For when fists beat thighs, eyes squint, shoulders lower. For when breathing stops, neck whips, torso rockets, joints lock, heart swells, and voice screams.

The Novice

I have to tell you I did not beg for the tickets. Somebody
at my father's work gave him a pair and said, "You
have teenage girls; they're gonna want to go to this."
I knew there was this group and this song "I Want to
Hold Your Hand" because my friends were going to do
a thing at the school talent show—you know, Kathy as
Ringo and Barbie as Paul—and I knew they all shook
their heads WOOOO! when they sang, but I was the
only one of my friends who got to see them in person . . .
if you can call it that.

My dad wouldn't take us, and my mother didn't drive
in the city, so her friend drove my sister and me to the
Civic Arena. It was sold all the way around. I remember
them coming out in gray suits, alone—this was before
the Jumbotron and the lights—and they were just
specks on the stage.

I can't tell you their set list, but I'm sure they played "I
Want to Hold Your Hand" and "I Saw Her Standing
There" because they had that WOOOO! which we all
knew was when we would clap and shake our heads
WOOOO! and then everybody would scream. Even
the fathers knew it was time to clap and scream. Really,
forty-five years later, my images are of the crowd to my
right, to my left, behind me, all screaming and shaking
their heads. I guess I just watched everyone around me
screaming their lungs out.

———

Remember, I was this fourteen-year old, from Blawnox!, with a wiener flip, village clothes, a circle pin. And fourteen then was like, way, way younger. Like ten now. But I wanted so much to be hip and cool. I wanted to scream along with everybody. I did try a few times, and my own scream got lost in the sea of other screams. And these people around me looked like they had this genuine need to scream and I wondered why I didn't. It was confusing.

But yeah. That was my first concert.

PART TWO

TIPS ON POPULAR SINGING

Space Oddity

AS I WRITE THIS, TWO RECORDS MADE OF GOLD are travelling out and away from me. They have been travelling since the year before I was born, when the planets made an agreeable path for chucking things out of our orbit. Each record is stuck onto the side of a space probe.

A decade after they left, one of the two space probes sent back a picture of us, taken from a 3.7-billion-mile distance; we were then a faint pixel of light on a long ribbon of brown against the black of space. That was over twenty years ago. Now that probe, record still attached, is one of only four objects crafted by us that have travelled past our solar system. And as of last summer, no man-made object has ever been farther from my grasp—or from yours, or from any living thing on this planet—than this spacecraft and its attached record.

The hope is that, in a few tens of thousands of years, the Golden Record will end up in the presence of a distant living thing, and that the living thing will find a way to suss out the pictogram that the humans at NASA etched into the record's cover. The etching tells the faraway thing to touch the attached stylus to the Golden Record and to spin it. In binary code, it instructs them in how to amplify the sounds embedded onto the record: sounds of earthly rain and thunder and of a beating mammal heart. There are greetings in ancient languages and in the language in which I type this, as well as whale language and bird language. And there are the sounds of man-made instruments playing fanfare and concerti, of drums in polyrhythm, and of two dozen popular songs sung by voices from six of Earth's continents.

A song like the "Kinds of Flowers" gamelan will illustrate to the faraway being how a human prince makes his presence known in a room, and a song like Mozart's "Queen of the Night" aria will prove that a perfect melody can court centuries of Earth's most powerful singers. The "Navajo Night Chant" explains to the faraway being that our young men must greet the darkness with the noise of their own unique power, while "Pygmy Girls' Initiation Song" shows how the happiest human girls are those who become women within earshot of a chorus of their sisters. The Bulgarian shepherdess song "Izlel je Delyo Hagdutin" tells the universe why a man would run down a hill toward men who want to kill him, while the Mexican *son* "El Cascabel" proves that a perfectly sung note can conjure a little bell, or a bird, or a lover, or all these things at once.

Only one song on the record sings to the faraway being in English. Another song is sung by a Texan, but the vocals of that blind preacher—about whom we know little more than an extraterrestrial would—are in no language, just rapturous moans. For English lyrics, the faraway being will only hear "Johnny B. Goode."

It made the Golden Record, no doubt, for Chuck Berry's mean guitar, but this guitar sound is not unique to Berry, and it did not begin with him. We hear verbatim riffs in songs from guitars that played ten years before his, and we have heard the same riff strummed in hundreds of rock outfits since. What *is* unique to the song is Berry's voice, the way in which he sings his story of a half-literate guitarist who dreams of trading his Louisiana cabin for a flashier space in the universe.

Will a listener from that great a distance be able to feel the parts of Berry's voice that so please the people of Earth? Will his flirty, upfront shout, his Midwestern pluck, and his forty-two repetitions of "Go!" on a waggish F survive the eternal voyage out? Will travel lessen the devil in Berry's trumpet voice, its cocky volley between wisdom and bluntness? And—perhaps the most pressing question of all—will they hear that shit-eating grin in his song, the timbre that makes all the best early American rock voices sound like they are strapped to jetpacks?

If the Golden Record can offer all of this to the space-bound listener, then Steve Martin will turn out to be right. As he predicted in a 1978 comedy skit, once the record lands in that faraway place, Earth will receive a return message, lickety-split. That four-word alien missive will be easily decoded and, within a week, the blunt interplanetary response will grace the cover of *Time*. The faraway beings will have written to us: "SEND MORE CHUCK BERRY."

Six years after "Johnny B. Goode" was recorded in a Chess Records studio, musicologist John Cohen climbed to a remote mountain village in Peru and found another voice that would end up in space. "Wedding Song" is a tiny *a capella* piece sung in Quechua-Inca by a girl of about fifteen. I'll wager I know as much Quechua-Inca as an interstellar being does, but I can hear in the girl's song what makes it worthy of a galactic voyage. Even after I've stopped the MP3, I hear her five-note melody with its teasing arc like a toe idling circles in the sand. It jumps up in a series of questioning verses, only to land flat in each three-note chorus: the catchy tune of a voice venturing a guess, then demurring. She sings in that impossible pitch that connects shy human girls to the birds in the trees above them.

Most alluring of all are the contradictions in her reedy performance. In the song, we hear her self-awareness of being young and shy, but she also sings with a wink, sounding funny and in control, and that discrepancy between timidity and power is what pulls me toward her singing. She sounds alluring and oblivious at the same time; she is Britney at high altitudes. I like to think her listeners from other planets would feel a similar attraction, and that they would holler back to her, to us, across billions and billions of miles: SEND MORE SONGS BY COY ANDEAN TEENAGERS.

The story of "Wedding Song" is a lovely foil for that of "Johnny B. Goode." Instead of rocketing to stardom, the girl in the song is trapped, and it is difficult to tell how she really feels about her situation. A man has tricked her into her own wedding (and wedding night), but she sings that he's only half to blame, as he was abetted by her own ignorance of the world: *When the rice fell on my head / I thought it was hailing (foolish me; stupid me) / When the house was full of people / I thought it was my birthday (foolish me; stupid me) / When we got into bed / I thought . . . you were comforting me (foolish me; stupid me).*

The melody wiggles a bit in its lyrical predicament; she seems to *enjoy* pretending that her lover has taken her under false pretense, too tickled (or too titillated) to keep a straight face. She is allowed to do this for thirty-eight fleeting seconds of the Golden Record, and then skitters out of earshot. Like all great girl singing sensations, she knows to leave you wanting more.

I know it will mean something to any faraway being that we devoted millennia to first charting our stars, and then to testing the hard facts of our planet so we could launch things outward to those stars. It means something to our history to have put great men and women in a room with the wealth of Earth's most prosperous nation, and that with this clout and funding and know-how they fashioned a 1,700-pound grasshopper that could speed to the edges of our comprehension. And it means something, too, to have put an object into the sky that can we monitor along with the sun.

But it means more to me that, once all the funding and red tape was secure, once the Voyager was loaded with its telemetry modulation units and spectrometers and radioisotope thermoelectric generators, we then made the decision to affix human voices to the contraption's flanks. And we added not just the voices of our leaders, but singing voices. And these were not only space-probe-caliber singing voices, and the music was not only Bach or Stravinsky. We also attached the cocksure gavotte of a twenty-nine-year-old hairdresser-turned-rocker and the shy aria of a mountain girl. This is what receives a first-class golden ticket aboard all that politicking and science. It beats out speeches and formulae and IBM and the *Ring Cycle*. According to NASA and Carl Sagan (and me), this is what we want the universe to hear.

Which is another way of saying that we have more faith in popular singing than in anything else on the planet.

The Soprano

At twenty-four I was teaching high school French in Indiana. I took a leave of absence and went to New York and never went back. I got straight to work: training, learning the arias, finding my Fach.

But I needed money. So I did the thing where you burst into the Equity auditions, sing your high C, get your card. This meant I also had to learn that "Broadway belt" and sing in musicals while I was still auditioning for the operas. One week, I flatted out in an audition. That weekend I found myself not able to sing every note of a choral score. Yeah. Trouble.

I went to one of the big voice coaches. He had a picture of Julie Andrews on his wall and, like, a dozen Annies who had come to see him whose voices were shot before they'd even hit puberty. I'm practically in tears and I tell him about bombing the audition and how he has to help me because I'm sure I've lost control of my voice and I don't know enough to fix it myself. And this guy was the top man in his field, so I'm sure he can cure me.

He turned and looked me straight in the face and said—and you have to imagine this thick Russian accent—"My dear, the voice is like a small dog. Sometimes is good dog, sometimes is bad dog. That is all."

JUDY! JUDY! JUDY!

[Music] cannot even be judged by the human ear alone,
since it is directed toward those immeasurably complex
and unpredictable psychological and physical reactions
of the entire human organism, and toward its qualities of
imagination and remembered experience.

—Ralph Kirkpatrick, "On Concert Halls"

I. OVERTURE: *"The Trolley Song," "Over the Rainbow,"*
"The Man That Got Away."

THEY WAIT FOR HER IN A HIGH-DOMED ELLIPSIS of unsteeled
brick and masonry. She is thirty minutes late and the Hall has filled
with their anxious fabric, perfume, and breathing. As they scan the
back corners of the red stage wall, they wonder if her singing sounds
the same. If it is still coltish and limber, like it was at the Palace in
'51, or on *Lux Radio Theatre* a dozen years before that. If she can
still belt, still swing. If she's as fat as they say she is.

Their eyes wander to the gap in the ceiling, the only change to the
Hall's anatomy in seventy years. Even the seat frames are the same as

that day in 1891 when Carnegie christened it "Music Hall," hoping to keep his name out of things. He hired an amateur cellist to design the shoebox-shaped room, simpler than the ladies of the Oratorio Society might have preferred: no gilded proscenium or frescoes. Its smooth-walled arch leaps over each velvet seat and shades it like an awning, like that famous phonograph cone into which the puppy sticks his nose. This is the Victorian equivalent of wiring space for sound.

The conductor starts his overture, the trumpets smashing through the one about the trolley, about the rainbow, about the man that got away. There is no bill of song; the programs in the audience's hands only say "Act One: Judy" and "Act Two: More Judy," plus a personnel list and an ad for Steinway. The full orchestral sound shoots from center stage, out past the vacant mic, and into the Hall, where it splinters. Each wave of the overture races to discover the hard surface it will hit first.

Those long and close walls make the music slap the sides of the Hall before it shoots up to the roof. Because the walls reflect sound first, the wavelength that touches the audience's right ears is infinitesimally different from the signal that goes left, deepening the work of the brass, reeds, drums, and strings. This small difference between left and right makes the sound bleed into other senses: the ticketholders can stroke it like fur, taste the flavor of it, wrinkle their noses at the musk it sprays. After bussing the walls, the music rocks up and then back to the carpeted floor, then fades into the curtained flanks, adding rhythm and even more shape.

We call that map of sonic travel the "presence" or "warmth" of this Hall, a hall that some call the first Stradivarius of American architecture. And though we may not know it, that presence is the reason we sit in the Hall, in any room, really, and wait to hear a voice sing to us. We're waiting for the moment in which sound fills a room and then changes from wavelength to wave: a thing we can surf on or drown in. A moment with undertow that hits us in the places where we move. Though, in these situations, we all choose to sit still while it strikes us.

The conductor looks offstage right, and there she stands. Tiny in flats, despite five inches of coif and a spangly jacquard wrap. Her brown eyes glisten with something wet, but he cannot tell if it is a Ritalin glaze or tears. She is twisting the fire curtain in her fists, tipping forward a bit into the folds of asbestos so that the front rows cannot see her. In her hiding spot, she shouts her trademark warm-up into the fabric. It inflates her, pump by pump, with each syllable. The conductor can spy on her from his podium. Though, at point blank range of the overture, he cannot hear her voice. He can only watch her tiny jaw mouthing the words of the warm-up: FUCKEM FUCKEM FUCKEM FUCKEM FUCKEM FUCKEM FUCKEM FUCKEM.

II. ACT ONE: *"When You're Smiling," "Almost Like Being in Love / This Can't Be Love," "Do It Again," "You Go to My Head," "Alone Together," "Who Cares," "Puttin' On the Ritz," "How Long Has This Been Going On?" "Just You, Just Me," "The Man That Got Away," "San Francisco."*

Her first concert was in a hall much like that of yours or mine: a little red-walled room that rarely seats more than one. Its acoustics are unparalleled. She lay, awash in sound, as voices and white noise traveled the scaffolding of her mother's tissues, skeleton, and plasma. Sound vibrated the length of her mother's spine, down through her pelvic arch, and into that snug listening room of liquid and muscle. There, it provided the most all-encompassing sonic experience a body will ever know, so powerful that we register it before we are even wired to open our eyes or make fists. Imagine the added power of that first hall if it were shoved under the keyboard of a movie house's piano every night, four shows a night. This was the bill of sound in her hall, from the day in the second trimester when she grew ears to the warm night in June when her father closed the theater to carry his wife to the Itasca Hospital.

She showed up having bathed for nine months in reprise after reprise of "Ain't We Got Fun," "Toot, Toot, Tootsie," and "(Tamale) I'm Hot for You." She was as expert in these melodies as she was in her mother's voice, the closest voice, the voice that boomed around her to prove the difference of a body at rest and a body in peril. Sound and emotion vibrated the fluid in any extra space around her. Lyrics lapped against her body; so did patter. She kicked to the sound of stop-time, vamps, and waltzes. She wiggled in the ripples of a dotted eighth note, and ballads slowed the beat of her heart.

Legend has it that, less than two years later, in the very same movie house, she first sang for an audience, yelling the only verse she knew of "Jingle Bells" until her throat gave and her father dragged her off. For a decade after, her tiny voice stretched its legs, first through every Minnesota social hall with a curtain and baby grand, then through the Twinkletoe Kiddie Revue, the Kinky Kid Parade, *Big Brother Ken's Kiddies Hour*, the Beverly Hills Pickfair, the *Los Angeles Examiner*'s all-star Christmas Benefit, the Second Annual Alfalfa Festival, the Vitaphone Kiddies movie shorts, and two weeks at the Chez Paree with Georgie Jessel.

Jessel changed her name from Gumm to Garland the year her voice broke. Weight and sinew had tipped it backward, dissolving the helium pitch of childhood, and then coaches built wind power and muscle strength around the hormones that waxed the cracks in her vibrato. By the time she sang "Zing! Went the Strings of My Heart" in the MGM offices, the test pianist had to run out of the room. He must have told Louis Mayer that from her tiny mouth came more sound than there was space in the office, and that it was still in there: a sweet warble banging the leaded windowpanes to get out. "The Little Girl with the Big Voice," they decided to call her, and they did, nearly as often as they called her the name that she'd christened herself: "Judy."

Tonight, this seventy-year-old Hall shakes when she leaves the wings and pump-walks to the center-stage microphone. New York women in organza slippers and kidskin gloves actually stand on the seats of their carpeted chairs to see her. But she begins the first song without a diva curtsy or the Jolson *pietà* arms, instead just skating out on the ease of the melody. The first phrase of "When You're Smiling" floats away, minus the showy *rallentando* wind-up of Durante or Louis Armstrong: *whenyahhsmiiileeeeeeeeeeeeeng*. Her voice swells and recedes with the long notes of the last two vowels, and that loose vibrato feels even more silvery in the treble of a mid-century mic. But the voiced lyric does not live alone in the Hall; it meets the voices of the ticket holders. So there, one electrified voice leaps into an SRO crowd and begets that crowd's choral push-back of deafening, unmiked sound.

Three thousand sets of cords touch 400 times a second, entreating the help of the whole body. Backs contract, ankles shake, feet tighten in wingtips. Each body is its own Hall as their physical architecture boosts the air in their throats, playing to their personal rafters, their crown molding, their buttresses. And as their bodies buzz with reflected sound, the Hall outside of them shakes further.

Variety will call tonight "the greatest evening in the history of show business," but maybe what happens has less to do with "show" than with the high-five between the crowd's roar and her infamous voice. They yell "Judy! Judy! Judy!" for her big sound, which can turn a Hall into that tiny red room to which we all had tickets years ago.

Dozens will report—in the *World Telegram*, in the *Herald Tribune*, and fifty years later in *Vanity Fair* and on NPR—that they wept a little with her first "When You're Smiling," shot from the stage like an arrow from a five-foot-tall crossbow. Perhaps they were frightened that, without the soft comforts of fluid and skin around them, this makeshift womb on 57th Street wouldn't weather such a full-bodied vocal event.

As she sings to them, they sneak wary glances at the ceiling three balconies above their heads, where the sound finally pools. The bridge in "When You're Smiling" turns into a medley, and she sings a rag-rhythm *Forget your troubles, c'mon get happy! WHEN! YOU'RE! SMILIN!* and they clamor.

Feel my heart, they say to the man on their right, and he does. Their chests hum with resonance from without and from within. *See?* they say. *I swear to Christ this whole damn place is gonna cave.*

III. ACT TWO: *"That's Entertainment," "I Can't Give You Anything But Love," "Come Rain or Come Shine," "You're Nearer," "A Foggy Day," "If Love Were All," "Zing! Went the Strings of My Heart," "Stormy Weather," "You Made Me Love You / For Me and My Gal / The Trolley Song," "Rock-a-Bye Your Baby With a Dixie Melody."*

When the set moves through a string of up-tempo numbers, she pounces on them, the drums racing to keep up like the back legs of a spurred horse. She meets the staccato wordplay of Cole Porter and Fred Fisher with a pleasingly baffled, Great Lakes response, like Steve Allen earnestly overpronouncing every syllable of "Bee-bop-a-lula." The fastest songs run their course in less than ninety seconds, the applause from the previous number barely waning by the end of the tune that follows, and their lyrics are often interrupted by the bop of her chin or shoulder pad on the microphone. Like the blaring horns behind her, she is somehow allowed to land on either side of her brassiest pitches in "Come Rain or Come Shine" and

"Puttin' On the Ritz" without doing any damage to the integrity of the melody. This turns each up-tempo song into a survival struggle, a bout from which she rises off the mat again and again, with style.

The ballads offer something else: a disturbing emotional vertigo, as if the floor is stripped down to a narrow I-beam that holds the sound, the space, and the evening together. She walks it solo, one note in front of the other, and they all hear her beckoning them to meet her, first at the bench she shares with her pianist, and then closer even, in the cabin of her open mouth. She whispers in and out of tune: *And I believe / that since my life began the most I've had is just a talent to amuse.* And then a flattening six final notes in mezzo forte belt: *HI, HO! If LOVE Were ALL!*

And then there are the swells in her end-notes. She builds little dwellings—caves, tents, awnings—in the bulges of the song, and the audience ducks with her into each new brassy schematic. In "For Me and My Gal," she tightens her grip on the swell, mimicking the musculature of a grin. She pushes her palate down for the swells in "The Man That Got Away," loosening the vowel, then rolling it from her teeth to her tonsils like a dram of Armagnac. She caps the "ah" swells in "How Long Has This Been Going On?" with strange punches of extra breath. After many swells, she puts a catch into the next note, like a hole in the floor she must step over to prevent herself from falling into the basement. The catches halt the meter each time, and she seems surprised by it, as if she has never sung "Come Rain or Come Shine" or "The Trolley Song" before. Her audience, in turn, is surprised by the sheer number of places she goes after catching herself. Dips, runs, trills, rolls—they never knew there were so many ways to be this loud.

Lenny Bruce isn't here, and he certainly isn't one of the hundred men who run down from the cheap seats after the finale. But he will play the LP pressing of this concert a hundred times, like nearly everyone with a hi-fi did in 1961. Later that year, he will tell another crowd in another kind of hall—one curtained and padded to make the acoustic dead-zone necessary for speech—that the Judy encore kills him. Not because of the way she builds three floors to "Rock-a-Bye Your Baby": first a lilting schmaltz, then a stripper-rhythm belt, and then a top-level so raucous she growls the last syllables. Not in how her voice, already twenty-three songs in, still flips and shimmies and blasts past the fire exits. Not even in those men at the stage reaching for her, shrieking right into her little face.

IV. ENCORE: *"Over the Rainbow," "Swanee," "After You've Gone," "Chicago."*

It's only *after* "Rock-a-Bye" that Lenny Bruce starts to pay attention, he says. This is after she has calmed the crowd underfoot, who beg her for "Swanee!" and "Chicago!" and for her to "just stand there!"

She looks out at the Hall and says, "I know, I know. I'll sing'em all and we'll *stay all night!*" At the prospect of being locked in the Hall with her until dawn, they all roar, and right then, she mutters to them at a half-octave drop, "I don't ever wanna go home; I never . . . ," trailing off. This is the moment that does Bruce in.

Because, he says, her voice falls out of sync at the word "home." This "home" she intones is not a showbiz exclamation, like the set list's songs of homes in San Francisco, Chicago, or Dixie. Here, the word "home" sounds nothing like the Kansas "home" Judy-as-Dorothy Gale sighed in Oz, or the Saint Louis "home" Judy-as-Esther Smith summoned after "Have Yourself a Merry Little Christmas." Tonight, "home," Lenny Bruce says, is no comfort, not in Real-Live-Judy's thirty-eight-year-old mouth. This home, to him, sounds "scary."

Bruce compares her low, stammered "home" to a child in bed, begging his mother for a fifth glass of water, not because he is thirsty, but because his room is built too flat, with far too many echoes and shadows to bear. He'll drink water all night long, though he is full and exhausted, rather than have her leave. Because a hand holding a glass to your lips is better than a dark, quiet room in which you float alone. Even if such a room is what we are all supposed to want, a place where thoughts can roam without accompaniment, without the need for performance.

Judy's muttered "home" reminds Bruce how foreign it feels—if you are a human like him or like Judy—to try to be close to someone inside the home, a house without rhythm or red velvet, without the amplified sounds of someone's hands or voice or heartbeat.

"Lotta *tsuris*," Bruce says of Judy, his voice shaking along with his head. "Lotta dues."

He might hear in her paid-up voice the "home" on Beverly Drive, where she escaped in 1950, two days after MGM fired her from a musical she didn't want to do in the first place. She locked herself in the home's master bath, smashed a drinking glass and sawed at her neck with the shards, as if to say, *Here! If this is what you want, take it out of me. Clone it. Fucking bronze it; I don't care.*

Or perhaps he hears in her "home" the cold tile of his own quiet room, where his housemate will find him, blue and naked with a cord around his arm, just five years after this show.

Or he might hear the cramped London home where Judy will live by the end of the decade. One June evening, she will lock herself into *its* tiny bathroom. Instead of breaking a drinking glass, this time she will fill one with water and slide far too many Seconal past her throat. Six hours later, when her fifth husband climbs through the bathroom window and lifts her body, it will moan at him a little, though it will feel hard and cold to his touch.

Or maybe Lenny Bruce hears the sterilized walls of the Westminster Hospital, where the on-duty pathologist will scalpel a Y shape into Judy's torso days after her death. He'll follow either the Rok-itansky or the "En Masse" method of autopsy, both of which take the larynx fairly early. Both require him to use his thumbs to sepa-rate the muscles that connect larynx to trachea, like popping beans from a pod, until he holds her voice box in his hands. He will then tie a string around it, lifting it out of her neck and placing it next to her on the table, so that it hovers outside her body like a droopy balloon.

In the pile of offal to be burned, he will leave the two white porous tabs, tinier than baby teeth, which hung on the walls of her throat for 572 months. They are a few millimeters larger than they were during her days on the MGM lot, slackened from cigarettes and Blue Nun wine, from encores and rage blackouts and bad pat-ter and orgasms. They will not make it across the pond to the Frank E. Campbell Funeral Chapel, a room of spartan plaster on Madison Avenue with pews for two hundred. Regardless, over ten thousand people will wait to walk past her last white metal box, which she will, of course, leave uncovered to let in the light.

There will be velvet walls—blue, this time—and glitter. And at eleven p.m., the Funeral Director will ask police if they can keep allowing people to pass through the threshold. He will leave the doors to the chapel's hall open long into the warm night so that peo-ple can stay inside and, in silence, answer Judy's hand-sewn mouth.

The Contestant

My Mom had been after me to audition forever. I was living in New York, super depressed, auditioning nonstop—a shit-ton of almosts—and then in February it just dried up. I was twenty-eight, which, as you know, is the cut-off age. My Mom called and said, "If I get you a hotel with my Marriott points, will you do it? So— literally kicking and screaming—I went to the Philly audition.

At some outrageously early time, we took a cab to whatever Philly's big coliseum is and stood in the parking lot. There were cameras everywhere and more people there than you have ever seen in your life, holding signs and wearing costumes, and all of them were singing. *They wouldn't stop, because they thought someone from the show might hear them. After, like, seven hours in line, we all took a seat inside the coliseum, and we filled it. Then we spent four more hours in the sun, listening. You should have heard the sound echoing in the hallways when you went to the bathroom—we're talking Crazy Town, population one thousand.*

Down on the floor of the coliseum were like twenty tents with open tops so you could see down into them from the stands. In each little tent was a person behind a table. When your section was called, you'd line up in front of one of those tents, wait your turn, step up, and sing. You could hear everybody auditioning around you—Aretha over here and Bieber right next to you. Can you imagine how hard that would be if you didn't find your pitches easily? And every once in a while, someone would come out holding one of those Golden Tickets, which only got you to the next round of coliseum auditions. The part with Paula and whoever was still days and days away.

Some people would go into the tent dressed as, you know, a crayon, and you'd hear them blow out their voices, and when they'd come out, they'd be waving their Golden Ticket, and the whole place would boo! Even the people way up in the stands who couldn't see anything would boo, too, because they knew there was some guy down there who was going to get on TV because he was dressed as Wonder Woman, so BOOOOOOOOOOOOO! It was the best part of the whole process.

Personally? The whole time I knew I was going to get down there and sing my face off and they were going to say "nice" and then that would be it. That's pretty much what happened. I sang the last verse of "Magic Man," the woman stopped me and said, "Thanks, but you're not American Idol material." I was like, boooool-shit I'm not Idol material! I mean, I'm a trained singer who knows how to sing a little rock, but she meant I don't have a story and therefore I am not made for TV. So that was it. And when it was over, I felt fantastic. And it shut my mother up, which was a major plus.

Hey Big Spender

THE HIGH C, OR C6, IS THE 64TH KEY OF A PIANOFORTE, the third-to-last fret of a classical guitar, the 36th string of a concert harp, and the highest usable note of an operatic soprano. To produce a high C with an oboe, one must apply nearly twice the air pressure used to inflate an automobile tire. A double bassist must drape his body over the front of his instrument, stretching past the forty-inch fingerboard and pressing the soft swell of flesh at the side of his thumb into the steel of the G-string, turning the skin and bone into a makeshift fret. His thumb inevitably splits and calluses.

These are all the same note. Like all notes, this C is born a straight line—of gut, of nylon, of air—and then cut into fractions. The result, when correctly executed, is a sinusoid that crests and troughs 1046.5 times each second. And though attack, decay, sustain, and release all meld to build unique envelopes of timbre around each instrument's high C, each perfect C6, no matter the device, subjects the listener to a compact piece of musical space. This space's power comes from the personal manner in which it is kept from growing further. Change the space too much, and you've burst straight through into the next note, an altogether different space with its own set of properties. So, there in its tight cage, a perfectly tuned C buzzes with a hummingbird's ferocity.

Soprani do not "hit" the high C; they "have" it, as if the sung C is a fretted notch on the cords of the body. Coloratura, Soubrette, Lyric, and Dramatic roles occasionally feature Cs sung on open "ah" sounds—*pacem, quando, alba*—but, more often than not, the C comes wordlessly—a high-flying "ah" on the tail of an ascending trill.

Even when sung as vowels, the note C sounds the way a letter C looks: a long and voluptuous curve with a serif bite at both ends. The note chooses this sonic identity over the shorter sounds of C in speech: the spit of breath that is "cordon," *caponne*, "Callas," or *machismo*. The thick trap that starts "cherry," that frames "church," that bridges "butcher." The sinister grip of "slice." The hiss of "seduce."

Eighteenth-century soprano Carlo Broschi, known only as Farinelli, had the C6, as well as the note above it, both of which rang through a Europe that valued loud, clear vocal tones in a much more visceral way than we do now. Back then, a song sung live was much more understood through touch and through feeling. Notes were not judged as simply in or out of tune; they were expected to be potent. To grip the ear, tease outward, then push back against the swells of each sine wave. Eighteenth-century theorist Angelini Bontempi likened a well-shaped high note to a shot of holy semen that impregnates the trained ear with a kind of sacred "agitation," a disturbance for which, in the afterglow, the ear's owner quivers with gratitude. Such worshipful listening began, of course, in the Church, where women had been forbidden to make joyful noises since Paul's letters to the Corinthians.

Some four thousand Italian boys of Farinelli's epoch entered church-sponsored music schools when their young voices were still high and bright, in an era in which sacred music grew more complex by the season. By the time of Farinelli's birth in 1705, Italian composers had borrowed decadent ornamental scaffolds from the Dutch contrapuntalists, because why build a simple ladder to the Lord after you've learned how a staircase can spiral? Baroque melodies grew to wander and waver, slowly dizzying up the central octave and, when reaching it, pressing out toward the next. A few dozen bars of this circling sound creates a desire for payoff. In the gut, there blooms a hollow reach for a top sound that is both glittering and justified, like an angel on a tree. Because of this infernal ache, that top note, when experienced, feels like a blessing from the highest conceivable place.

Mastering these complex new lines required years of training and a thoracic power that exceeded even the strongest and most gifted of choirboys. By the time they learned the proper technique for possessing the ecstatic C6, most of them would have already descended into baritones. So, sometime before his tenth birthday, Farinelli was laid into a warm bath. Too young for laudanum, someone pressed their thumbs into the line of his jugular, cutting his circulation and thus sedating him, while a second pair of hands made an incision in his scrotum and popped his testes from their sac. Or perhaps the hands reached into the water, ran their index fingers along the anemic cord that looped around each testicle, fretted it, and then lanced it. This would have caused his unremoved testes to retreat home to his abdomen and, eventually, fade away.

Italian fathers, farmers, and country veterinarians repeated these processes for over two hundred years, the curtain of secrecy drawn more closely in some provinces than in others. But the sin of unnecessary dismemberment was punishable by excommunication everywhere, so the altered boys all came to choir ready with excuses. It was most fashionable for gelded choirs to blame their injuries on swan bites or, in Farinelli's case, a horse-kick to the groin.

In the 1750s, every last one of the soprani in the Sistine Chapel was an alleged victim of a wild pig attack.

Farinelli's body continued to change long after his genitals healed. The joints of his arms and legs stayed soft for most of his teens, allowing his appendages to stretch freely, like stalks on a long reed. His fingers and neck became unusually long as well. He won considerable height (his nickname was "the tall F"), soft skin and, perhaps most importantly, a broader ribcage. Unhindered by the gonadotropin that tells calcifying bones to stop, the curve of his ribs kept curving at a wider arc. This, with training, allowed his lungs to billow like a damper. A cathedral for the breath.

At the time of Farinelli's fateful bath, his vocal cords probably measured about seventeen millimeters. Barred from the glands that would have eventually fortified them with testosterone, those marooned cords stayed small, bearing the hit of each scale, etude, and rudiment without changing. The years of conservatory rigor yielded seventeen millimeters of the most pugnacious, flexible tissue a human has ever built. A pair of acrobatic, seventeen-millimeter terriers crouched at the top of the larynx, refusing to grow even to the size of an adult woman's. But who needs women when a man can sing this high, and with this much power? Who knew any human could stretch and burden a muscle until it shouldered rooms full of air pressure, like a worker ant lugging a crumb ten times its size?

Imagine waiting in your cold pew through the exposition, development, and recapitulation of a florid theme. Anticipating musical resolution has proven to speed the currents of blood that vibrate the strings of our bodies. And then, thank God, that wait is halted by a top note rocketing from Farinelli's young mouth, riding a cannon of hefty and reassuring air. The air holds his note aloft for half a minute, plenty of time for a congregational exhale. This is the blueprint of a pontiff's C. A C for kings. A C that Charles Burney called "clear and penetrating." A C that flautist J. J. Quantz called "very fertile."

And a C that, soon enough, forced itself to burst from the church that made it.

Less than one percent of *la scuola dei castrati*'s graduates made the leap to the great opera houses of Europe, where men could not only sing like women, but portray them, too. Farinelli and other superstars of his class became the human embodiment of the balls-to-the-wall *opera seria* for which most of polite Europe was rabid. Critics noted the delicacy with which the Tall F, as Adelaide, grasped his fan and touched his thin fingers to his carnival masque. Due to papal law, he sported trousers underneath his hoop-skirt.

But these were not men simply bred to play women. At the height of their popularity, composers who favored the castrati wrote for them a new heroic archetype: the Incorruptibles. These roles are otherworldly men (often kings) who endure epic hardships through an unflappable belief in goodness, or in moral fiber, or in the power of true love. Job in the fifth octave. A little later, Handel imagined castrati as the most virtuous and godly of lovers: the weepy Orlando, the fawning Bertardio. Gluck scored one of Greek mythology's most passionate lovers, muse-born Orpheus, *a castrati*.

No matter whom they portrayed—Abel the good shepherd brother, a paramour-cum-butterfly, a disembodied soul spiraling to heaven—the roles of the "beardless men" challenged even these top-notch voice athletes. Castrati arias remain some of the most demanding in the western repertoire. Because the singers had buffed away that cavernous break from chest to falsetto voice, composers ran staves wild with coloratura passages—sections of song alarmingly dense with notes at close intervals. Francesco Araia's *Berenice* includes the castrati role of Demetrio, who, in a quick and violent "rage aria," sings 30-measure-long chains on the "va" of *precipitando va*, and the "fa" of *Ch'impallidir lo fa*, all while staggering up and down three octaves of the scale.

But the more ambitious the libretti, the happier the gelded divo, and Farinelli's composer brother Riccardo Broschi wrote the humdinger of all castrati lines. In Broschi's contribution to a 1734 version of *Artaserse*, Farinelli found his Suitcase Aria, which he trilled while chained to a garish set in Covent Garden. From this performance, his *messe di voce* became continental news.

To perform a single-note *messa*, the voice begins in a cocksure mezzo-forte. A few bars in, the note slowly retracts, sliding back from the hollow concert hall, decibel by decibel. Still on the same breath, it thrusts the note into the room again, full forte, in a seamless punch. The result adds motion to an already perfect tone, so that it penetrates the ear, then nearly quits it, only to push back in again with a heightened intensity. And it takes *forever* to happen, a slow and delicious torture. The trick could make an audience feel vertigo, as if the earth were moving underneath the orchestra pit. Thus, with this *messa,* the Tall F literally rocked the house.

The surprise command with which he manipulated the note—his long arms were bound at the wrists as he sang it—was so thrilling that one London blueblood shook in her box till she had to sing herself. The papers reported her performance right alongside the singer's—the way she hollered to the top of the hall, over the scuffle of the crowd, so fucked with high, tight, spiraling sound that she forgot what was charming in a lady.

"One God," she screamed, "One Farinelli!"

All this aural hanky-panky happened in the 1730s, when a castrato seemed capable of magic. Farinelli, in one of the earliest reported art therapy sessions, sang the chronically depressed king of Spain back to health, earning a knighthood for his troubles. Other top castrati, many of them born far below the aristocracy, rode to their singing engagements in the coaches of Flemish, German, and English duchesses, and often commanded enough in performance fees to eventually purchase their own cooked-up dukedoms. Imagine fine society peppered with these courtly, curt giraffes, well-schooled in manners and fashion from their years in the theater, advancing into top status thanks to their experiences *playing* top status.

And that's not all they stole from the amorous characters they portrayed; there were rumors of the other things young geldings were taught in those Neapolitan singing schools. Though last century's endocrinologists ruled that anyone castrated before the onset of pubescence would grow up impotent (or, at least, sexually unmotivated), back in the 1700s, all castrati were tigers in the sack. Rich (and usually married) patronesses courted and pampered the singers, as did more than a handful of their husbands. A smaller few even had public relationships with monarchs. Cassanova himself wrote in his memoirs that he once found himself enamored with a castrato—one who belonged to a cardinal, no less—but he and his apologists insist the singer must have been a beautiful woman in pants.

Gossip rags and theater columns carried rumors about duels between castrati and the husbands they cuckolded. At least three fictionalized accounts of Farinelli's love life appeared before his death in 1782 and, though the real Farinelli was never linked to any romance, all three of these fictions were riddled with sexual intrigue. Other castrati enjoyed perpetuating the lascivious buzz. Senesino, the top castrato until Farinelli outsang him in Handel's opera house, once published a saucy monologue stuffed with double and triple and quadruple entendres about the women of London, all of whom "hankered" after his "tree that gives no fruit." To satisfy an enlightened woman, Senesino hinted, only your notes need be potent.

So perhaps it wasn't just fame or skill, but also this fruitlessness that led to a continent's obsession. In their sterility, castrati provided an opportunity for fantasy that was both exotic and safe, like the pleasures of music in a framed and controlled hall. Women could imagine a lover—graceful and tall, well-dressed and soft-skinned—who satisfied all of his conquests, but brought with their pleasure no risk of conception.

Or perhaps the appeal was in their otherness. Maybe the doyennes of London spent their afternoons imagining how a set of alien fingers, long as tapers, might feel on their throats. How the fluttering of a castrato's *fioritura* might sound right next to the ear. What parts of her a Tall F breath might shake if it were exhaled from underneath a lacy canopy, or, better yet, a set of panniers.

Or it might all just come back to the C. One can't underestimate the shock of a "female" voice on a Baroque stage, even if Farinelli made his London debut fifty years after Nell Gwynn did. And to hear that girly voice escape the concertmaster's staff and push into secular, structural ecstasy must have felt like a peep show from behind the veil. In Farinelli's highest note, they might have heard a terrifyingly private sound, one usually made by a woman, smirking at them from the mouth of a breathtakingly lovely man. Maybe the women felt anyone who sang sounds so close to their own must understand the root tone of the noises women make.

Did men feel the same way two centuries later, upon hearing a square-jawed, shoulder-padded Lauren Bacall hit a baritone C3 for "put your lips together and blow?"

By the end of the eighteenth century, the music world had stretched again. Farinelli had been outsourced to the Spanish court, and then into retirement. From his Bologna rooms, he spent the last few years of his life giving audience to the young turks of music, including a teenaged Mozart, who for years spoke with wonder about the alluring castrati tone that old Farinelli demonstrated. And in Mozart's last opera, a powerful and otherworldly "Queen of the Night" bursts from her cave in Act Two and backs the ingénue into a corner. She then sings a quicksilver rage aria that features eight piping high Cs in a row. And at the end of that line is a legendary ascending phrase that winks twice from a fourth above the C—the ribald, agile, superhuman F.

By the time "Der Hölle Rache" debuted in Vienna, that F6 belonged to a woman—Mozart's sister-in-law—and Farinelli was nine years gone, buried with his cloak of silk and his Spanish sword with a jeweled star. Nearby were the trappings of a pop star's life: a half-dozen royal harpsichords, a pearl guitar, a Stradivarius, a menagerie of animal paintings, "flotillas" of manuscripts, a coach, a carriage, six mules, and an indeterminate number of Hungarian horses.

They unearthed him in Bologna in 1810, after the Capuchin monastery that housed his crypt was ruined in the Napoleonic wars, and again in 1850, so that an insistent grandniece could share the crypt. And in 2006, a team of forensic anthropologists dug him up a third time. The cloak and sword were nowhere to be found, and what was left told them very little about the sound of Western music's most famous gelding: twenty-five sturdy teeth, a porous clavicle, a long slim ulna with two matching femurs, an unusually tight pelvic notch, an unaccounted-for set of worry beads, and one straight, white rib.

After the unification of Italy, castrations were outlawed; nevertheless, the Vatican did not issue a decree banning new castrati from their chapel choirs until 1902. Popes before then had been hesitant to place an outright ban on castrati, perhaps for fear that parishioners might stop coming to Mass altogether. Still, even after the ban—and even after Italian women were permitted to not just sing, but to train as rigorously as men—the Vatican kept its own stash of castrati. The last of the Sistine Chapel boys, Alessandro Moreschi, began his career with the same storied slice around the time of the American Civil War. Four decades later, his career ended with a different kind of cutting.

London's Gramophone and Typewriter Ltd. visited Moreschi in 1902 and entreated him to sing the Gounod "Ave Maria" into a hollow tube. At the tube's terminus, a tiny diaphragm flexed and retracted as Moreschi's voice altered the atmosphere around it. The pressure of this change then shook a razor-sharp stylus that, in its motion, divided a beeswax cylinder into long, thin lines. After Moreschi sang "Amen," the cylinder was dipped into a bath of chromic acid, so that it would sing that same way forever.

This "Ave Maria" is an easy-to-find MP3, and many call it the only castrato voice to which the twenty-first century has access. This is disappointing, as Moreschi's odd, cracking performance wouldn't incite anyone to either scream God's holy name in a concert hall or to break the vows of matrimony.

Plus, in the early 1900s, recording technology was as young as Moreschi's voice was withered. And Moreschi wasn't ever a celebrated castrato outside his home region, or even a particularly well-trained singer; he was really more an altered alto than anything. Such bad timing yielded two scratchy, faint minutes of unsexed whistling. But because this is the only specimen that found a sonic taxidermist before his breed's extinction, his is the voice we can visit.

One of the clearest notes of the Moreschi recording is the highest one, sung at the final *hora* of *in hora mortis nostrae*. It is a long note that the old man manages to trill and sustain, peppering the sound with just enough shake to stir some excitement in the listener. One might just think, for a half-measure, that this dry voice could satisfy us, as he holds the note aloft and curves the sound upward in an all-too-true line about the hour of our death. Maddeningly, though, that hopeful top note falters right at its close. Worse still, it's a B5.

The same year as Moreschi's geriatric "Ave," tenor Enrico Caruso strode into a room rented by the Victor Talking Machine Company and fired off ten arias at ten pounds per take, leaving with the equivalent of ten thousand dollars for less than a half-day of singing. He commanded this beefy fee because the Victor A&R man had a hunch. He thought Caruso's massive tenor was a cocktail of pitch, force, and grandiose expression that could overshadow the considerable shortcomings of early recording. In 1902, contemporary equipment often couldn't detect the notes of double basses or celli. But Caruso's explosive tones, inching up the fourth octave to the new power C, the C5, not only registered on records; they could help early phonograph owners forget they were listening *to* records.

When Caruso's voice warmed the tin recording horn into which he placed his whole face, he ushered in the era in which notes fill spaces independently of the bodies that sing them. No longer did a C need the church, or Covent Garden, or a chancellor's ballroom to thrive. Caruso's C could come home and put up its feet in any common parlor. His became the first voice in our history to go platinum.

Among Caruso's very early recordings is "Ombra Mai Fu," from Handel's version of the *Serse* story. One of the most recognizable pieces in the Western repertoire, few know that this aria (also probably the first music ever to be broadcast) was written for a castrated voice. Handel's favorite male soprano, Cafferelli, would have opened the slow vocal line with a *messa* on C5. From there, as the Persian king sings about a plane tree he encounters on a walk, the melody paints itself with slow languor, like streaks of loose clouds. Up in the fifth octave, the castrati-pitched line wafts over the chord changes like the sun coming in and out of hiding, aping the shadow imagery in the aria's short lyric: *A shade there never was / of any plant / dearer and more lovely / or more sweet.*

But in the tenor range, "Ombra" is earthbound, closer to the instruments that accompany it. It peers up at the shady tree from down near middle C. Caruso's warm notes are cut thick, like planks, and sung with the communicative vigor of an adult man's speaking register. In the Caruso recording, we hear the stops and starts in his chest and the heavy consistency of his reinforced vibrato. And the strongest top notes—three F4s in the final six measures—are not so much meteorological, but rather meteoric—as if a circus strongman in a singlet were lobbing cannonballs into the fabric of a big top. We wait for them to fall back to the circus floor, and that waiting period is a frightening and perfect human moment. All the lauded tenors of the twentieth century—Lanza, Di Stefano, and a bit later, Pavarotti—chased this vocal persona: The Italianate Lyric Tenor, the raging bull of the C. This was what a modern man sounded like—in the opera, at least.

But sometimes the notes did not make it all the way up. In his twenties, Caruso's Bflat4 often broke in public, and audiences in the lesser theaters of Europe and North Africa called him "the Glass Voice." After blowing the doors off the Mercadante in 1895, his unsteady Bs and Cs drew whistles and hisses in Barcelona and Budapest, making him so nervous that, in Trapani, he drank before a production of *Lucia di Lammermoor* and switched the all-important lyric "fate" with the word "fox." It was a scandalous gaffe; he was dismissed without pay and had to dodge young street toughs that followed him through town, shouting "Volpi!" "Volpi!"

It wasn't long before a maestro named Lombardi got hold of him, and of what the papers called "*the* B-flat," which Lombardi set like a femur. He worked all possible modulations of the note, then moved on to the B and then to the dreaded C that had so often weighed his young pupil and found him wanting. They spent a year welding each note to the throat, and then they stuck it to the less touchable muscles.

You have not read enough to sing the C, Lombardi told him, and he sent for novels and notebooks. *You have not travelled,* he said, *and when you do, you spend all your time sleeping or out with the chorus girls.* He took him to Greek temples, and he all but timed Caruso's meals. *Stop wolfing down your supper; between that and smoking you'll beat your tonsils to death.*

What torture it must have been to bow down before a note, after besting a childhood in the slums of Naples and three years in the army, as Caruso did. To be the first of his mother's eighteen children to beat infancy; to debut in Europe as a performer of hot blood and moxie, already a big shot with a full change of clothes. And then, at twenty-four, to be cut back to homework, field trips, and reminders to keep his fat elbows off the table.

And what must it have been like to sit still while this battered bull tenor sailed through *Il Trovatore* a year later, knowing full well he had been brought to his knees, cuckolded even, by the very note he was about to perform? How could a voice that mighty ever sound humbled, the crowd must have thought, when he began "Di Quella Pira." In the last syllable of *o teco almeno corro a morir*, Puccini planted a C5. Through Caruso, it is sung in the voice of a mountain that collapses and then shoots lava back up at the sky.

Like Farinelli, Caruso's virile tones led to unprecedented stardom. They also sparked mutterings about his body and what he did with it. His heavy vocal cords dangled an eighth of an inch farther down his throat, people said, and his mouth had a half-inch more girth than it needed. *And have you heard that he could puff that gargantuan chest and use it to push a piano from one end of a room—with carpet!— to the next? Or that the Frisco earthquake happened hours after his* Carmen, *because he sang loose the earth around the opera house?*

In Atlanta, Helen Keller visited him between performances; she put one hand at his throat and another right into his ominous "ah" mouth, as if he were the stone *Bocca della Verità* and she were a tourist telling it something true. Even Keller couldn't stop talking about his steamroller voice, which she touched as it "swelled and surged in harmonious billows." He had sung her the weepy aria of loss from *Samson and Delilah* (of course). According to the *New York Times*, "the voice of the tenor stirred her" to the point where the woman nearly fainted.

And oh my goodness have you heard how, in every opera house he visits, he catches the prettiest chorister, kisses her in the dark, and then kisses one of the homelier girls "for penance"? And did you know the woman singer we all thought was his wife that left him for a Lithuanian count wasn't his wife at all? And did you read about him pinching a woman's bottom in the Bronx Zoo monkey house and then blaming it on the monkey, whose name was Knocko?

By the time he was infamous enough to sell out bullfighting arenas, the Caruso C was a sort of burlesque number. He would inch to it from the frequencies below, *nearly* embrace the note, and then flat a bit before trumpeting, C! with full tenor fury. Toscanini chided him for grandstanding, but this in-and-out tease worked well with German and Latin American houses, which particularly enjoyed the punishment of a loud flirtation.

And added to this sexy uncertainty was a live, of-the-moment fear that something in Caruso might break, right before their eyes. Audiences vied for seats closest to his preferred marks on the Met stage, in order to watch his face and neck seize up as he sang. A chunk of vein would rise the length of his forehead, throbbing with stymied blood, splitting his reddened frontal lobe in half. This is where their delicious fear lay, in the possibility that so much heavy lifting might implode before them. *Can he do it again? I heard he still hasn't stopped smoking those Egyptian cigarettes. My God, look at his cheeks; they're purple!*

Even his internal doubt was no secret. "I never step on the stage without asking myself whether I will succeed in finishing the opera," he wrote of his seventeen hard seasons at the Met. He felt relief, he told one reporter, only after the last note of every evening left his throat. One night, even that was too presumptuous. During an elaborate curtain call, he was dizzy from the long performance, and he bowed his way backward into a scenery batten. Then he staggered backstage and blacked out.

CARUSO'S INJURY SERIOUS, the *Times* reported, SINGER MUST ABANDON HIS ENGAGEMENTS FOR SOME TIME. This headline caused a panic, until the same newspaper sounded the all-clear a few weeks later.

And for fifteen years, any doctor's visit was written up like a natural disaster because "a permanent impairment of his voice [would] affect four nations." After hearing of a performance at the Brooklyn Academy of Music during which he actually began singing blood, readers didn't relax for weeks, until the *Times* covered Caruso smiling and waving on the ramp of a launching ocean liner. "To show that his voice was in good order, he ran up the scale a little to a 'top C'," the *Times* reassured readers. But soon again, the headlines were bold-faced and terrified.

THE TENOR FORBIDDEN TO TALK, SO DELICATE IS HIS THROAT.

His Only Hope of Being Able to Sing Again is in the Surgeon's Knife.

CARUSO BUST IN SILVER; Singer Offers It to Saint Whose Aid He Seeks to Recover Voice.

BLOOD CLOGS VOICE; He Wipes Away With Handkerchiefs Before the Second Act.

CARUSO BURSTS VESSEL IN THROAT; OPERA ENDS.

The payoff of all that hyped terror was a pleasure not even the castrati could offer their audiences. By creating decades of doubt, Caruso then had the opportunity to consistently dismiss that doubt, performance after performance, boat launch after boat launch. And each time he did, the mighty C looked down from its final perch in the catwalks, chiding, *Now don't you feel silly for worrying?*

Caruso peppered the first fifth of the twentieth century with impossible, Spruce Goose Cs, each thrown into the air with the grunting output of a clean-and-jerk, and for that, the nation was grateful. They were so grateful that they chased his train car, stretching their arms to his window so that they might touch the walking stick he held out to them. One might argue that their love for him was so deeply felt because Caruso presented himself as an underdog, a fighter who clawed his way back to the top notes. But it could just as easily be said that his audience—descendants of those crowds who shouted "long live the little knife!" at Farinelli's cut kind—were out for vocal blood.

Because there is a certain kind of artistry that, at its most superheroic, blends skill and expression into a performance of ultimate expense, and we have taught ourselves to crave that dangerous art. Another way of saying this is that we expect man's highest and most beautiful notes to be costly, and we are excited to swoon at the high price tag. It is sexy to think that another person has given his life (or his gonads) to make a perfect note, or that he is killing himself in front of us just to get the music out of his mouth.

Because the C will raze a man's throat until it bleeds, until, in the last eighteen months of his life, it fills the lining of his lungs with toxic fluid. One Christmas Eve, after a final performance of *La Juive*, he will draw a warm bath to ease the ache in his side and then lie down in it. Then, there will be a rip inside of him that makes him holler loud enough for passersby eighteen floors below to shudder. The C will force a surgeon to break one rib, then another, and insert a long knife into his spleen until the bad liquid bursts from the cavity in such an explosion that it slaps the doctor like a glove before a duel. The cut will stay open for several months until, in August, the C will finally take him down. He will draw his last big breath in the city of his birth, and then they will lay him out in a hotel named after the world's most famous volcano.

The Phoenix

*They took the cords and sliced them down to these thin
little wires and they replaced the rest with tissue from
some blood that they'd frozen. They knew they had done a
remarkable job—there was a pretty good chance that I'd
never be able to speak again—and so they woke me up in
post-op and said, "Look at this elegant work!" I remember
thinking, "Oh, just give me more morphine."*

*I stayed on vocal rest for a month, but then the band had
booked a tour of Italy and I had to honor that. We can't
all take a few years off to rest like Springsteen. So the first
noise I made after surgery was singing. Soon after we got
there, I was coughing up blood.*

*I came back from the tour and my voice was all fucked up. I'd
fade halfway through shows; I had no muscle memory at all.
I almost had to reprogram my body to work the vocal cords.*

*And this was hard, because I had never separated my voice
from my interior life—it never felt like something that I
had to conjure up. When I felt like singing, I did it. Maybe
that's what happens when your Dad puts headphones on
your little baby head and lets you listen to* Sticky Fingers
*all day long: you never think about the right way to sound
because you don't isolate it at all.*

*The most frustrating part was there was no character, no
texture to it after the surgery. It was a scary kind of clear.*

It took me ten more years of really intense therapy and training to get the rasp back like I wanted it. I know that sounds fucked up, but quality is relative, right? I'm not trying to hit all the right notes when I play. Sometimes I don't think I sing the same note twice in one night.

And Your Bird Can Sing

The idea was originally just to write . . . songs that a Crow
would sing. In other words songs with no music, in a
super simple and a super ugly language which would shed
everything except just what he wanted to say.

—Ted Hughes, 1971

SOME BIO-ACOUSTICIANS BELIEVE IT WAS SONGBIRDS that
inspired early humans to try their hands at melody. Because way
back then, in birds, we could hear how sound might entail more
than just howling or beating out rhythms with sticks. Sit in an
outdoor spot long enough, especially at dawns or dusks between
April and August, and you'll get direct lessons in why. Birdsong
carries variation and counterpoint, theme and melisma. In the
bird vocalists, there is proof that a line of sweet, trilling notes—the
longer the better—produces a shimmering and obvious pleasure,
one unlike the thrill of an object bluntly struck.

The oldest known handcrafted instruments were flutes, which,
according to recent unearthings in Germany, we made 35,000 years
ago. Their sound approximated the reedy tones of a songbird's
syrinx through a similar system of air and piping. With these

short cylinders of vulture bone or mammoth bone, we made the first tunes for dance and ceremony. Then we probably used them to teach our bodies to sing. But unlike birds, we did not keep on singing just to advertise that we had not died in the night. We sang, instead, about things that got us *through* the nights—celebration and folklore and prayer.

Soon after, we strung gut across wood; a little while later we scored in gymel and fauxbourdon. This begat "O Lady, the Birds Right Fairly," "four and twenty blackbirds," "tu-whit, tu-whoo, a merry note," "A Nightingale Sang in Berkeley Square," and "Skylark." These then led us to "Blue Jay Way," then "Tennessee Bird Walk," then "Bird is the Word," then "Surfin' Bird," and then "Free Bird."

In the fairly recent past, we decided that the songbirds are "vocal learners" like us, a couple other primates, a few species of bats, and maybe the elephants. We call all these species "advanced" because they learn to sing outside the egg via a gloriously detailed adolescence of listening, hormonal ripening, and trial-and-error. Once a bird has learned his song, his tune holds a cachet unique to both the bird and his perching grounds. He *is* the specific song he sings, even if it is difficult for the human ear to pinpoint how his songs differ from his neighbors'. Some songbirds, like the canary, even learn a new song at the beginning of every mating season, to associate themselves with the hottest trends in music. All this personalization could be what inspires us to make our own songs in the tradition of birdsong, as the sounds of ourselves ringing against the changing world. Maybe this is why we sing so many songs *about* birds—to remember the perfect pieces of nature that first inspired us. And maybe it is also why forgetting the feel of daily birdsong is such a lonely and dehumanizing thing.

Take, for example, a prairie winter like the one in which I am currently mired, one whose January frigidity I've strained to shake off straight through February and on into March. Under the lead apron of this Iowa winter, I have no capacity to envision the months of mornings that brought to my window a dense and knotted mass of birdsong. A marathon winter is a trial of memory. As certain kinds of light and smell are sucked from my experience, I catch myself trying to will into view a tree with leaves, or the feel of air through a screen door, or even the demarcations of the parking lot, which were erased weeks ago by the ground-in snow. You know a winter is especially harsh when you find yourself pining for the spartan lines of parking structures.

For me, however, sound is the sense hardest hit by the long winter. I can sit by this window all day without listening. Unless I play my records, there will not be a single line of music. If cars pass, I hear the shush of their tires in the snow, but no songs from their radios. No ice cream trucks, no City High Marching Band practicing on the field five blocks west of here. And no birdsong.

I try to rally. I take walks and hum. I pass a quarter-acre of white lump and recite, *Here is where Amelia plants her garden, and last June you lay on old sheets in the fresh air and sang to her squash.* I walk between the giant sooty banks that the snow plows push from our roads and say, *Here is where Kansas played the college homecoming and sang fifteen obscure songs before finally doing "Dust in the Wind."* Or I drink in a bar where the jukebox is turned down for the TV, and patrons curse you if you hold the door open. There, I forcibly remind myself, *Outside that very door is a patio where, just six months ago, you sang a Blondie song for jukebox karaoke. You were wearing shorts and a tank top with a blackbird on it.* From these efforts, all I am learning is that song disappears further when forced into little stories.

There have been bird noises—caws and hoots and the occasional screech—but very little birdsong. I would say that I missed the thrushes and wood-pewees of eastern Iowa, but like the feel of the grass in Amelia's garden, I can't recall enough about them to be specifically bothered by the loss. Plus, something else has taken birdsong's place.

My landlady has hung a dozen feeders from the stripped trees, and she's cut trenches in the snow so she can fill the feeders every morning. But since January, the only birds that visit have been crows, and I know this fact displeases her. For some reason, my yard has become a hot spot for swarms of them, dozens more than the five or six that passed through last winter. I've never seen crows bigger than these Iowa crows. It's as if they saw how huge Iowa hawks could grow and then decided to compete. They are reckless and unpredictable guests, just like the trickster crows in Aesop, and I love watching them do bad things all over the lawn, clucking and bickering as they walk in twos or tag-team squirrels or butt each other from the ledge of the water trough that my landlady fills on above-freezing days. Like most yard birds, they come off as busy and diligent, though their agenda seems much less good-natured than that of a goldfinch or thrasher.

My cat, much more prone to scheduling herself than I am, never misses the crows' morning visits. She sits in the ledge of my basement apartment's window, which is level to the yard, and waits in her benign and declawed manner for one of the murder to wander close to the pane. When one does, she tilts her head and the crow does too, and they hold each other's gaze in a way that seems to worry only me. A beak's length and a slab of glass separate them, and I marvel at how they match each other in size and weight and stillness: one black, one gray, one with wings and the other a tail. The crow all but shuts his eyes, while her eyes get much bigger. It occurred to me, at the end of a cat/crow showdown, this was the one rare moment that a crow in my yard was silent.

Their voices, dampened by the storm windows, first sounded to me like the barking of dogs: a gravelly yip-woof on repeat. I initially heard these early voices in rough outlines, blunt as the shapes of their dark bodies in the December snow. Back then, they were little more than a misdemeanor annoyance, like waking up to an unfunny radio Zoo Crew or to the sound of the garbage truck in reverse. But soon enough, the cat and I grew attuned to the ins and outs of the crow outcry.

I now hear the difference between the crows squawking for their intimate crew and their put-on vocal airs for more distant kin. The rapid whoops made by a few crows in the trees now sound nothing like the sound of a mob of crows calling for reinforcements. Right before they leave the yard for the day, the crows perch on wires over my car and shit. When the wind is out, they will bleat a *vivace* stream of flattened notes, but they trumpet longer sounds if the day is still and bright.

"Crows mate for life, you know," said some guy at the bar the other night, and then I heard the clucks and struts of each marriage. I looked up the species, and found that their calls are divided into over a dozen categories—"assembly," "duet," "frustration," "premortality or death"—and now I think I can hear those sounds, too. And then there are the most arresting sounds. Every ten days or so, I'll walk by the window and find them—what seems like *all* of them— in the yard at once, yelling a chorus in the trees and on the ground, voices joined, their tails fanned out flat. This is when the crows are at their absolute loudest, their necks extended to make straight lines with their backs. From this position, they trumpet upward and outward with very little finesse or regiment. During these reckonings, it does not sound as if they are distressed, or celebratory, or amorous, or defensive. They just sound loud—as if, in this moment, the loudness is all. They swoosh their tails and scream up to the sky, and whenever they do, the cat turns from the window sill, her green eyes as big as they ever were, as if to say, *Holy shit. You never told me anything alive was allowed to sound like* that.

•

But I do not think the crows have held my attention all winter long simply because there are so many of them, or because they are so noisy. I think they have my ear because they are the principal agents of motion—both visual and sonic—in these dozen dead weeks. We've had two blizzards so far this year, and my boyfriend's car is frozen into the gravel. Everything around us is still and similar. As their crow voices get closer to the center of my brain, so does my desire to reach out to them and listen further. I'm like an infant straining to bop a mobile because it's the only thing in her fuzzy sightline that sings and spins. And the more I look and listen outside my window, the more I hear of their spastic black-and-white movie, as chirpy and raucous as *A Hard Day's Night*.

On a recent morning, both the cat and I stared out the window for what felt like hours, watching the loud scene of a crow convalescing, and eventually giving in, before a jury of his peers on the lawn. Disoriented and woozy, he made a staggering descent from the wires above the roof down to the snowy ground. His carriage lacked the sleekness of most crows. His feathers sprang up in rumpled swatches, giving him the outline of a pained vagrant hunkering into a patchy frock coat. When he pitched forward into the water trough, I couldn't stand to watch him any further. I left the window and rinsed the breakfast dishes, trying to croon to myself. When I came back, the cat was asleep and the crow was face down in the brittle snow.

Above and around him, the murder traded voices—those loud caws in a pointed, but still indecipherable, syncopation. Were they brainstorming? Yelling a plan to remove him from the yard? Were they mocking him or mourning him or pointedly trying to ignore him, making sure that Creation saw how well crows cope?

As they hollered, the dying crow's claws curled like witches' shoes under a house. This was the most dramatic scene a bird had ever offered me.

•

Americans have sung about crows nearly as often as we've sung about songbirds, flying them through two centuries' worth of lyrics about courtly devotion, the seasons, and flappy dancing. Since its founding in 1894, *Billboard* magazine has listed scores of popular tunes with "crow" in the title, like "Sly Little Crow" (trad), "I Dunno Said the Crow" (1917), "Two Crows" (traditional), and "The Blackest Crow" (1899). My favorite might be "The Song of the Crow" (1905), in which a crow bachelor is first rebuffed by his girlfriend for not being able to croon like a canary, then accepted because his "harsh and rough" noise "comes straight from the heart." But the melodies themselves don't sound anything like the crows outside my window.

Nowhere in popular crow song is the sound of the rumpled crow who died on my lawn. Nowhere is the sound of the Iowa riverfront on February evenings, when a hundred crows roost in the black, bald trees, so that the branches seem to shake with the buzz of their intimate clucks. Rather, each human crow song's tune seems inspired by the sounds of the "real" songbirds— jangling and catchy, with the lilt of whistling and flight. For centuries, in our parlors and dance halls, we sang about crows not in their loud language, but with the voices of nightingales.

We also don't seem interested in sampling crows the way we do other songbirds. There are lines of (imagined) woodpecker vocals in Kay Kyser's "Woody Woodpecker" (*Billboard*'s seventh biggest song of 1948) and an entire dawn chorus, with its swoops and spirals and conversations, in the Kossoy Sisters' hit version of "I'll Fly Away." There is three-part tweedle-dee-dee-ing in "Rockin' Robin" and clips of actual birdsong in "Groovin'" and "Blackbird." In all this radio free birdsong, nowhere do I hear the rash shouts and guttural accidentals of my yard birds.

In 1953, a harmony group called The Crows had the fifth most popular song of the year, a pitch-perfect doo-wop number called "Gee" that, sadly, has about as much to do with crow sounds as the following year's "Sh-Boom." But who could blame the Crows for refusing to mimic the sounds of their namesakes? There was no precedent established in radio for anything more than straight-up song. And on either side of their Billboard Top 20 spot were adorable ditties, glassy as a slow river in the sunshine: "Moulin Rouge," "You, You, You," and the Mitch Miller colossus "How Much Is that Doggie in the Window," one of a half dozen top 40 hits to feature loud barking.

Long before we began recording songs about animals, we decided that crows did little more than bark like these doggies in the windows. We grouped their noise not with the vocal-learning songbirds, but with the voices of the majority of the animal kingdom—innate, imprinted sounds. Crows, we decreed, were born cawing, as cattle were born with moos in their mouths. This also means we thought that the caws of crows had nothing to do with the sounds that inspired our cave selves to sing.

I assume American music fans might say Elvis was the first pop idol to make the sound of the crow when he crowed in 1956, or maybe that Little Richard predated him while crowing through "Tutti Frutti" the year before. This is because they sold a million copies making sounds that are dirtier than Doris Day's or Eddie Fisher's or even Muddy Waters', thanks to the loud, unpretty finishes that ice their most dramatic notes. And yes, these vocal moments do sound like crowing. But when "crow" is a verb, it refers to a different kind of bird. Both "Hound Dog" and "Rip It Up" are chock-full of *crowing*—that preening and raspy cock-a-doodle-doo that brings with it a sun-up regularity. They rock, but it is metronomic rocking. Their crowing is like a porch chair, a back-and-forth to match the righteous pound of a boogie-woogie left hand.

What's more, both Elvis and Little Richard are still singers, over-all—still more crooner than crow. They wed melody with repetition and dynamics to make our ears feel wooed and sung to, even when they awopbopalula. Their 45s prove they can flip, with ease, from crowing on one side to crooning "Send Me Some Lovin'" or "Love Me Tender" on the other. This is the beauty of their sound, especially early on: we hear the melodic payoff of pairing church noise and sex noise, of marrying the jagged to the well-oiled. But none of this is what a funky, capricious crow would do, had Sam Phillips perched him in front of a Memphis mic in 1954.

I say the first pop chart-topper that sounds anything like the crows in my yard is the Fendermen's hophead version of "Muleskinner Blues," which reached number 5 on the *Billboard* Hot 100 in 1960. The country standard about the plight of an out-of-work cowboy was written thirty years earlier by Jimmie Rodgers, and its tune was well known for its elastic runs of pretty yodeling. Singers from Merle Haggard to Dolly Parton to Odetta have recorded its long tones and big jumps from chest to head voice, but in 1960, the Fendermen refused to sing it even remotely how it was written, abandoning its melody (and, for some phrases, melody altogether) to make two minutes and twenty-three seconds of addictive trickery.

Over two wobbly guitars plugged into one amp, and with no drums to fence him in, vocalist Phil Humphrey half-sings and half-burps Rodgers' lyrics, cramming any guttural resonance he stumbles upon into the loosening structure of the song. He growls, laughs from his throat, lurches into falsetto, and at varied points quacks, mewls, honks, hee-haws and bock-bocks. He doesn't yodel because he cannot, skipping the scalloped leap from chest to head and instead using his gut to push the notes from low to high. The tune wavers, then poops out under the weight of Humphrey's spazzy glossolalia, and we forget that there ever was a muleskinner—or maybe even a Jimmie Rodgers—by the last measure, a snide "cha-cha-cha" barked by Humphrey and partner Jim Sundquist.

Fifty years later, we've relegated their tune to silly song compilations, but there's more to the Fendermen goofy noises. Yes, their work is all very cartoony and undanceable, but it is also so very loud—louder than Elvis's crowing, and at least as loud as Little Richard's. It's also much more denuded. At several points, you can hear Humphrey step away from the mic so that his shouted notes don't feed back into the mix. The more you listen to him go at it, the more the other voices in your playlist sound palsied, foreign, and still. I've found that, when the mood strikes, I can spend an hour staring at my track screen, zoning out to the bumps and clucks of "Muleskinner" on repeat.

According to their website, both Fendermen were twenty-two in January 1960, the month they cut "Muleskinner" at 7½ speed. The northern Minnesota rec room in which they recorded was a thousand miles and at least two decades from Rodgers or any mule train. It could be that this distance from the lyrics is what led Humphrey to make such joyfully horrible sounds.

Or was their impetus the weird hush of late 1950s pop airplay, legless since Elvis left, crystalline with frigid hits like "A Summer Place," "Running Bear" and "Volare"?

Or could it have been Minnesota in midwinter, months past the departure of its birds and music, that prompted this noise? And maybe then that motionless winter spread the Fendermen straight through the thaw, from the basement to tiny halls in the Upper Peninsula, to stations in La Crosse and Saint Paul, and to another studio in Minneapolis. Then it crept into featured nights at the St. Paul

Auditorium and the Val Air Ballroom, and finally, at the last minute, onto the Great Lakes leg of the Johnny Cash tour. That first night out with Cash, the Fendermen walked onto a stage and faced 10,000 fans yelling for "Muleskinner." They did not sing, not at first. The two college juniors saw the gigantic crowd out there in the black, then turned to each other, dumbstruck. Then the boys guffawed—an awful sound at full volume—straight into their microphones.

·

Recently, we've changed our minds about crows, reruling that they, too, are vocal learners. We now place them (and their cousins, the ravens and jackdaws) in the Oscine suborder with all the famous birds that sing of spring, of the dawn, and of human popular feeling. This regrouping rules that every crow in my yard has a personal and acquired voice, and that every last one of them is, at least in terms of taxonomy, just as much a songbird as a robin or bluebird is. So it turns out I've spent this winter listening to singing all along, to birds that can treat noises like notes and the air like staff paper.

What's more, we now know that crows learn a speech that is remarkably fluid and transmutable, even surpassing that of most others in their order. They have dialects and localized catchphrases. Sometimes, a foreign crow will find that he cannot speak the language of the crows around him. Each small nation of crows learns and evolves their own deep lexicon of community calls, volumes, pitches, and—especially—rhythms. Many zoologists think we can use these varied phrasebooks to conduct our deepest inquiries on how (or if) other species create art or culture for themselves.

And to top it all, in 1979, biologist Eleanor Brown published a study that said crows do, in fact, "sing." Few discuss this particular crow noise, however, without putting "sing" into quotation marks, as the sound of this "song" is so very weird and unable to regulate. According to Brown, juvenile male crows (who enjoy longer adolescences than most animals do) string their childish babbles to create extended lines of rhythm, tone, and fuzz. They use it as idle group noise, like street corner doo-wop gangs did in the 50s. Their process mirrors the "sub-song" stage of traditional songbirds, another teenage phase. But a crow's "singing" does not seem to come, as most birdsong does, from a need to communicate sexual prowess or general safety. Teen crows "sing" like we do: to get to know one another, to pass the time, or to shoot rowdy sounds out into the long, cold days.

And perhaps most impressively, spectrograms have revealed that all ages of crows speak in whispered pitches too low for human ears. They use these pitches to speak to their intimates, or even just talk to themselves. They murmur this low talk as babies, and in adulthood, they use it to say kaddish for their dead. As if a subterranean musical between these young *bêtes noires* has been staged, right under our noses, for centuries, and we never knew it. Or as if we once could hear them singing so low and primal and, over the course of the relevant past, we forgot how to listen.

Maybe this is why we wrote crows into our folklore as scavengers and avengers and harbingers of death: because their near-silent rumblings *did* speak to the dark and avenging parts of us. Just as bluebirds sing of the prettier songs inside ourselves, crows might "sing" a version of our own dirtier, idler music. Or at least they reach the parts of us that listen with instinct. After all, until Lucy's hyoid bone stretched an extra centimeter and dropped into the cradle of her adult larynx, humans had no power for speech or song, either. Her sounds were little more than yelling, clucking, or babbling because, for several million years, man could only crow, too.

·

Growing up, I first thought music must be melodious, à la Garfunkel and Gaye and McCartney and Ronstdat. The two songs I listened to the most in my first twelve years of life were "Daydream Believer" and "I Feel Pretty." But then, because everyone else in the seventh grade bought a copy of *Nevermind*, I did, too. I put it in my tape deck to keep up appearances, gritting my teeth through the first few listens of "Smells Like Teen Spirit" until I became gleeful about the mush-mouthed accidentals in Cobain's vocal delivery. Through those harsh listens, I found myself reconditioned to the point where I could hear him more deeply.

I found power in the way his half-sung notes crashed into the rolling, three-instrument fuzz that accompanied them. I then moved on to the baleful, insane noise he makes in "Something in the Way" and his cover of "Man Who Sold the World," or in the ranting rasps inside my friend Mike's barely-audible, thrice-dubbed copy of Nirvana's first tape, called, I believe, "Fecal Matter." The more I listened to Cobain, the more he sounded like something worth listening to, but I never felt like what I was listening to was singing.

The same goes for many vocalists who, though they recorded before him, I discovered after Cobain. One would never compliment, for instance, the "song" of The Clash. While Joe Strummer and Mick Jones (both wiry slumpers with inky black hair) created two of the most powerful albums of the twentieth century, the noises they make throughout *London Calling* and *Combat Rock* are not exactly singing. They chant, they incant, they croak, and they most certainly crow, and all of this makes music, but not song.

Several other bands that fascinate me sport brooding, hulking front men, but lack lead *singers*: The Troggs, The Birthday Party, The Kinks, The Dismemberment Plan, The Modern Lovers, The Chrome Cranks, The Cramps, The Cure, The Stooges, The Faces, The Small Faces, The Gories, The Pixies, The Velvet Underground, The Monks, The Animals, The MC5, The Sonics, The Ex, The Fall,

The The. My adolescence became a circuit of this strange practice: first the initial audition of these human crows thrusting sound from their throats, and then the slow peeling through their delivery, past melody and form, to reach what lies beneath them. For forty years of pop, we've heard interjections from these nonsingers and their voices, which are often called "primal": screams and hollers and stutter-step articulations, sounds aerated by whiskey and smokes, scattings and mumblings and slantings of the mouth so that the air rushes out in a sneer.

I'm not saying that all hard rock sounds are tuneless. There is plenty of feeling and merit, and maybe even melodic technique, in a raw delivery. Tom Waits rattles, Mick Collins caws, Patti Smith brays, and Corin Tucker screeches, and all their voices make a definitive sense. I suppose I'm saying that their musical logic is the logic of the crows. And if these loud, wrong sounds were to fully overtake recorded human song, half of me would miss traditional voices: Jo Stafford and Maria Callas and Smokey Robinson and Lata Mangeshkar. But the other half of me can't help but insist that lovely noise should never be the only "song" of our species.

Sure, some subjects were obviously made for the songbirds: golden childhoods and gentle sex and summer sunshine. Their inverses are the topics most often heralded by pop crows, but even the sweet subjects of pop can sound better when screamed or shrieked, or belted out a half-step sharp. And in the wintry climate that is postnuclear airplay (or web-play or satellite-play or whatever mess we're in now), some sentiments cannot be sung as prettily as others. Would I really want to hear a trained tenor like Caruso sing "Masters of War"? Would Nat King Cole do justice to "California Über Alles"? What would happen if the Vienna Boys' Choir tackled "My Ding-a-Ling?"

And how exciting it was to hear woozy, possibly tone-deaf Sid

Vicious snatch the honeyed line of "My Way" from Sinatra? Sinatra, with his ironed cuffs and suite at the Sands, could never be a crow like Vicious. I'd wager that Sid's *only* individual contribution to music was that cover of "My Way." In his throat, the song becomes a hideous dirge about prefabricated stardom, or Enoch Powell, or garbage strikes, or something. Ditto for Blixa Bargeld, whose terrifying "Over the Rainbow" somehow retains the doe-eyed wonder of Garland's version, but with an opiate wink toward the truly fantastic.

Gritty rock vocalists, like a swarm of birds in a suburban yard, hide things from us, or at least from the parts of us that just play music while we commute home or sit in a bar and throw back shots of Cuervo. They tell us, in no uncertain terms, that there is weather that asks for colder noise with more darkness and less frivolity.

•

It was the crow in Bob Dylan at the Manchester Free Trade Hall who looked up at the heckler and smirked, just as it was the crow inside the heckler that yelled "Judas!" in the first place. Standing there in his dark and fuzzy suit, Dylan knew what was being asked of him. In response to the man in the balcony, he whanged the crust of each vocal end-line so that it soured the resting measure that followed. He drooped at his neck so that the syllables fell from his face like marbles. He turned to the Band, his eyes slits and his beak cocked, and rattled at them to make a mess of the last song of the set. "Play it fucking loud," he burbled, in a voice so low it drowned in his monitor.

•

A few days ago, I was walking to work in the early morning, and I heard my first songbird of the year. We've still yet to melt around here. Spring is something you think you smell on certain afternoons when the clouds are close, but then you see the gray light and wonder if you aren't just fooling yourself. On the way into town that day, I had passed a sundress in the window of a boutique on Dubuque Street, and I found it ridiculous, as was the thought that my arms would soon be, or ever were, bare.

The bird was absurd, too, singing solo a few paces away from the English building in a tiny whistle. Undergraduates hustled beneath him in their ruined Uggs, most of them with small buds impacted down in their ears. His was a neat little trill, back and forth between two short runs of notes, maybe a chickadee or finch. But I didn't know what to do with his song.

Those blooming whistles ran such a countermelody to the light and the landscape and the icy air in my chest that they were difficult to hear. And when I drifted to the memories of the riverfront crows and that slow death of the crow in my yard, I felt myself relax in their familiarity. It was then that I realized that, had someone told me a story that referenced "bird," these would be the first images I would summon. Not the blue jays of my youth or my favorite birds, the cuckoos. Not the bird sounds my grandfather taught me to whistle: bobwhite, whippoorwill. Not the Iowa owls I hear *in flagrante delicto* each May. Not the ibises and egrets of the swamp where I played as a girl. Not the little brown sparrows after which my family is named.

After seventeen weeks of winter, this was the flashcard in my mind when I summoned the word "bird." This was the sound clip, too: a placeholder for the dark and satisfying voice in my ear. The word "birdsong" was a lyric, a stand-in in for the gravest of images: a hulking, rocking body, a barely visible mob, a fucking loud singer that calls you from your window and out into the snow.

The King

When I did my very first show out in Georgetown? No
musical background before that. Nothing. I mean, I never
even sang "Happy Birthday." I said to my wife, "It's sink
or swim," and then I just went up there—sold-out crowd,
250 people—and I made a damn fool out of myself. At
one point I said, "Now my next song's gonna be 'Love Me
Tender' and I heard a lady in the audience just go 'Oh. My.
God.'"

That's when I thought "Hmmm. Maybe I better learn
how to sing." So I just started listening to Elvis all the
time. That's one thing that I do that a lot of the other guys
don't—I listen to Elvis every day. I do. A lot. It's a habit. I
also watch a lot of YouTube.

Now, the crowds all start sweating and pass out. They fall
on the ground turning around and crying or they sit there
bawling. Last time I played the birthday concert at Chuy's,
a lady stood out there holding her Elvis sign, cried and
cried through the whole thing. I said, "It's all right, Honey;
you don't have to cry on me. I understand."

I've had people in the audience accuse me of lip-synching,
which some of the Elvises do, but not me. I'll say, "Yeah?
What's your name?" and then I'll put on another song
and I'll say their name while I'm singing it. I usually get
little kids coming up to me to say, "You're not really him!"
or "Elvis doesn't drive a minivan" or "You're dead!" But

then I'll do the voice: "Well, if I'm dead, how am I still here talking to you . . . RIGHT NOW!" That can make their eyeballs move out their heads sometimes.

Yeah, I do feel like I'm him when I'm all dressed up. Not that I claim to be him, but, I mean, you better believe that you're Elvis when you're out there on stage, 'cause that's what they're paying you for. You're being paid to be Elvis. And hey, man—I give 'em what they want.

Teach Me Tonight

> Whether it is a ballad, a hill-billy, a swing number, a novelty
> song, a marching song or a comedy number, the popular song
> has that special something which makes people forget their
> troubles and cares. . . .
>
> —"Tips on Popular Singing," p 4

PREFACE
(and *A Word of Commendation* by Tommy Dorsey), p. 3

IN 1941, THE EMBASSY MUSIC CORPORATION printed "Tips
on Popular Singing by Frank Sinatra," a short text—little more than
a pamphlet, really—by the singer and his coach, John Quinlan.
"Everyone can sing a little," the manual insists, assuring its reader
that "the popular vocalist, who has had voice training, beyond a few
simple exercises, is the exception rather than the rule."

Sinatra had just broken Bing Crosby's six-time streak as the
Downbeat vocalist of the year, and *Billboard* had bestowed him
with a similar title. He was the solo vocalist of Tommy Dorsey's
orchestra, the top band in the nation, and his "I'll Never Smile
Again" had held at number one through the previous summer and
fall. He was twenty-six and did not read a note of music.

Even though, decades into his solo career, Sinatra would sometimes declare that he never took one voice lesson, most confirm that he spent his early twenties working on and off with Quinlan, an Aussie Bel Canto tenor fired from the Met for drinking on the job. The Sinatra that arrived at Quinlan's apartment for his first one-dollar lesson was shifty and marble-mouthed, but his voice had spirit. It carried the post-teen passion of a spoiled but driven music nut who had already decided a) that something inside him deserved to be heard and b) that popular songs were the only way he could make a big enough noise to satisfy himself.

Even as a Hoboken nobody, Sinatra had ideas about singing, gleaned from a lonely childhood spent worshipping both radio and the musicians that passed through town on the way to New York gigs. Though his young voice was tight and much less expressive than the voice we now know as his, Sinatra had already begun straining toward a sound that was cufflinked, pedigreed, and better-than. You can hear this in the apprentice-level sounds of his first recordings, before Quinlan. You hear the American songbook squirming inside his neck, excited to get unstuck.

Quinlan began by training Sinatra's body from feet to pelvis to neck to temples, remolding it as a reservoir for polished tone. His breath was inflated to accommodate long, smooth notes with constancy. The mouth that, in speech, wrenched itself into Joisey knots was reprogrammed into masks of widened, relaxed singing positions. These masks—a face for every phoneme—were cross-referenced with different modes and shifts in melody, which made all Sinatra's sounds blend into one another.

By 1941, five years after his first lesson, the Sinatra sound figure-skated out of the nation's radios, a presence you knew to be his at the first note, a flood of lacquered sound. The thirty-two-page "Tips" claimed it could work similar magic on any interested body and face, for just seventy-five cents.

GENERAL INSTRUCTIONS, p. 5

The first lesson of "Tips" is an embarrassingly easy one. "It is suggested that the student listen to the records of as many different vocalists as possible, take, for instance the Vallees, the Columbos" and—though it could've gone without saying—"the Crosbys." Sinatra met Quinlan already having completed that first day's homework; he was the rare child of the 1920s who had not only his own bedroom, but his very own Atwater Kent, at which he knelt every day after school. A Bing Crosby poster hung over his bed. By the time he was sixteen, singing local weddings and rallies for sandwiches, the neighborhood knew him as the skinny doofus who swanned about in Bing chic: yachting caps, ascots, pipes.

Crosby was a sensible choice of idol, as he, more than any other crooner that "Tips" cites, made Depression-era radio more exciting. The first crooners embraced that miracle of twentieth-century sound, the studio mic, by singing in low and heartfelt styles, countering the blare of the bandleaders or the busy vaudevillians. While Jolson, Durante, Prima, and Calloway shouted to fill noisy halls, early radio sheiks Vallée, Columbo, and especially Crosby sang close and ornate, as if the screen of the radio speaker were the lattice of a confessional window.

As Bing and company popularized singing in close-up, Tin Pan Alley heated up crooner lyrics, to the point where they bordered on purple. By the time Sinatra met Quinlan, many writers were composing lines too schmaltzy to sell with a straight face. "Tips" also mentions singer Bob Eberly, who uses a mayonnaise tenor to gloss over lines like "To me your voice is like the echo of a sigh / and when you're near my heart can't speak above a whisper," and handsome Jack Leonard, Tommy Dorsey's top voice until Sinatra took over, whose forthright, hunky baritone takes the sting out of turgid lines like "you are the breathless hush of evening / that trembles on the brink of a lovely song." The lesson here, in both Eberly and Leonard, is that to stay afloat on these new crooner lyrics, you needed to get a strategy.

VOCAL EXERCISES, p. 9

"Tips" devotes most of its pages to sixteen chromatic passages, sung in fragments of near-gibberish, which the pupil is to repeat again and again to build the muscle memory of his breath, face, and cords. Many witnessed Sinatra singing a few of these exercises, like "let-us-wander-by-the-bay" (number three) and "that-is-all-for-to-day" (number sixteen) into his seventh decade. Some passages are weirdly food-obsessed, like exercises seven ("eat-your-beans-and-bar-ley-too") and ten ("give-that-boy-some-bread!"). Other lines smack of the same heat that wafted from Sinatra's boyhood radio. Exercise fourteen, for example, could be from a prewar ballad: "the-night-is-long / and-you're-so-far-a-way," sung in scales to the tune of a chiming clock.

In order to sing exercise fourteen properly, "Tips" coaches the singer down to each twitch. To both make a beautiful noise and sell the sentiment of the line, he must use vowels as his ballast:

> Begin with just a little mouth opening on the word THE, and open wider on NIGHT. The word IS calls for a small opening, with the upper and lower teeth barely touching each other. . . . Open again on LONG. . . . Then, after taking a breath, sing the word AND with only a slight mouth opening, and hold this position until the end of the phrase.

As the lips expand and contract, they create an audible passion. Try speaking "the night is long and you're so far away" the "Tips" way yourself, making sure to change your mouth shape as per the above instructions. See how the long-sung vowels of NIGHT and LONG showcase the evening and its endlessness? Feel how the tighter mouth gives the last six words a receding clench, as if the distance between the singer and the "far away" sung-to are too painful to articulate with a full throat?

Such phrasing is the first major pillar of Sinatra's Greatness-with-a-capital-G, because nearly every damn line of his discography, even in turkeys like "Mama Will Bark," is this full of color and nuance. His take on a song is always a joyride of shape and dynamics, caressing the sound at every turn,while cranking out perfect wavelengths of covered tone. Half the thrill of listening to him is in the surprise of the next wide or narrow or throaty or puckered syllable and how it mirrors the flow of a song's special story.

Sinatra sang these action-packed syllables with the attention of a good pupil for fifty years. He used the ballast "Tips" gave him to outlive nearly all his producers and collaborators, making "Tips" sounds past the birth of Rock and Roll and the death of Disco and the discovery of Grunge. He sang them alongside Fitzgeralds and Armstrongs and Clooneys and Davises, Jr., the Diamonds and Jobims and "King" Coles and Pavarottis, the Streisands, the Bonos. This "Tips" coaching is the exact delivery that shaped what is arguably America's longest singing career. It was a sound that was popular both for its refinement and for its ease: a girded, articulate, and balletic voice. And also, if we are to believe "Tips," a teachable one.

MOUTH POSITIONS, p. 31

At the end of the sixteen lyrical exercises is a page without any words, just five hand-drawn mouths making the shapes of the five vowel sounds: AYE, EE, UH, OH, and OO. A "Tips" singer is advised to treat each vowel as a fixed gesture, like the hand choreography in "YMCA." While Sinatra did allow himself to play with consonants—dropping *g*'s, fusing "*th*" into a street tough "*t*"—these five fixed mouths herded his vowels, keeping them ahead of the teeth to ensure crispness. It's an edict Sinatra heeded so well that his sounds are often mimicked as chewed. Find any tribute artist from Atlantic City to Branson, and the fake Frank's mouth will vogue through every vowel face on page 31 to sing "Fly. Me. To. Tha." and then end in the extended flex of the twin OO in "Moon." Because the vowels, all Sinatras know, are where the action is.

MOUTH POSITIONS: UH

Fig. 1

The UH vowel in "Tips" is a fine place to hear Sinatra separate himself from the crooner pack, as it was cellular-level choices like the ones in his UH that readied him, out of all the boy crooners, to best Bing. While Bing and his wannabes would open up for a tall and bright AH sound, Sinatra sang it UH, adding a pinch of guttural thrust. Where Bing Crosby would sing a plucky AH in "Too-ra-loo-ra," bumping the vowel ever-so-sweetly like an avuncular bassoon, Sinatra sang the "all" in "All the Way" with a kind of *unh-unh* bump that no one should ever associate with her uncle.

This is part of the joke of "Swooner Crooner," a 1944 Porky Pig short which portrays Bing and "Frankie" as roosters singing to the hens of Porky's Flockheed egg factory. At the end of the day, when the two have crooned acres of eggs from the Rosie-the-Riveter hens, the pig asks them, "Gee Whiz, fellas. Howdya eh-may-eh-may-eh-make 'em lay all those eggs?"

The roosters answer in unison, "It's very simple, Porky. Like this."

And then the Bing rooster—in a Hawaiian shirt, tapping a pipe—huffs a perfect "*ah*-boop-*ah*boop-*ah*boop-*ah*boop-*ah*-boop."

While the Frankie rooster—bow-tied and skinny as his mic—lets out a baritone bell tone "Uhhhhhhhhhhhhhhh!"

This is the UH of "Tips," nervy and romantic, almost pelvic. A fresh way to get a chick to lay an egg. You can hear the voice actor who plays the Frankie rooster follow the "Tips" advice to "not spread from ear" and to "pay strict attention to the jaw," which helps drop the AH tone to both the basement of the mouth and the sweet spot of the chest. Puffed up, stomach in, he might have even leaned away from the mic to douse the UH in thick Sinatra power.

Just as Bing's intimate croon awakened something in young Sinatra, that tiny change from AH to UH was punk enough to make young postwar listeners, flush with cash and hormones, take notice. So when Sinatra made the final word of "All or Nothing at All" a lofted F sung as UH, female listeners too young for nylons heard its new power, glossy as the curl Sinatra Brylcreemed to his forehead, and they heeded it. They ran to Dorsey Orchestra gigs, shouting through the instrumental numbers for more songs with that revolutionary Frankieee feel. And after absorbing that UH, his audience released a sigh so big that the Draft Board briefly classified Sinatra's body 2-A, as his singing was "Necessary to the national health, safety, and self-interest." That long, deep, sigh was not an "ah" of relief, but something else entirely.

THE ART OF BREATHING, p 7

A "Tips"-taught breather inhales as he normally would, but on his exhales, he yields his natural breath to the melody, holding out to please the phrasing of the song. This requires major inhale power, which Sinatra earned after dozens of hours of eat-your-beans-and-bar-ley-too. "Tips" coaches its pupils further, stressing that exhales can be jarring, and when they must happen, they should never produce audible air. In short, nowhere in a popular performance should there be breath that is not pulling melody with it.

This is probably why it is so rare to hear Sinatra breathe on tape. Breath, he once said, could murder a record. A microphone coquette, he'd swing the hinges of his elbow and neck in opposite directions, pushing the handheld mic close for "and did it . . ." but shunning it for the inhale, and then reeling it back only just in time for ". . . my way!" When he stood behind a mic, he asked that its stand be black, to fade into his suit. To guarantee he could outlast the long phrases, he swam (some say he even sang underwater), took long walks, played vigorous golf, and borrowed Tommy Dorsey's trombone trick of taking cheat swigs of air from the corners of his mouth when nobody was looking.

This absent breath was one of Sinatra's careful gifts—a rule he lived by, like wearing jackets and ties in Jilly's pool room. Erasing the breath united the song, the mic, the lungs into a unit, dissociating singing from everyday vocal work, like speech. On 1955's *Songs for Young Lovers*, the engineer only trapped a handful of air across all eight buoyant tracks. In "A Foggy Day" or "I Get a Kick out of You," he just leaves where there should be breathing—a disappearing act. Then, after the inhale, he returns to the song, grabs the listener by the wrist and tightens his grip—a trapeze man fresh from the bar.

So how might such a principled breather take Jennifer Holliday's center-stage lungs in "And I Am Telling You I'm Not Going," a song whose emotional stakes are miles higher than any in *Young Lovers*, and one whose title takes an entire breath just to say? At the 1982 Tonys, Holliday's breath is more a part of the show than anything. Miked in the wings, in the floor, in her hair, she can't escape it as her character, Effie White, tries to sing her way back into her career and into the arms of the man who has left her. Between each note of the song, she corrals air and presses it from her body in squalling buckets-full.

Her pantsuit bunches as she braces the stage floor; her makeup beads and her jaw hinges like a cash register all from the work of this breathing. The audience watches it wring her into knots. And as her fists punch more air into her mouth, she releases breath in sputters, chirps, and some of the most forceful notes ever associated with Broadway. They are dirty notes—sometimes flat or adenoidal—but, when phrased with these desperate, hulking breaths, they are strangely musical.

The house first goes apeshit for a ten-second belt with no break for breath, and then they lose their minds *because* she breathes: 266 seconds in, between the lyric "you're gonna love" and the last word "me," she devotes a suspended half-second not just to inhaling, but to stuffing six thousand cc's of air down into herself in an uncorked suck. It is the sound of a hero resurfacing after three minutes under treacherous waters, or of a dagger entering the heart of a Jacobean avenger.

The note she voices with that sucker-punch breath, a cheerleader-loud "ME!" that wavers in and out of tune, is meaningless. Because the breath is what resonates in the theater; it is the real music of the song's trite *rallentando*. It is the sound of a trained singer who knows that the only way to sing like a woman desperate enough to break any rule in the book is to break the major rules of singing, "Tips" be damned.

Thirty years later, singers who cover "And I Am Telling You" still gulp that last breath, as if it were scored on the staff alongside the fermata.

MOUTH POSITIONS: AYE

Fig. 2

Nineteen fifty-seven was a banner year for the vowel that "Tips" spells AYE and rhymes with WAY, and not just because Sinatra recorded "A(ye)pril in Paris," "Ba(ye)be Won't You Please," "The Night We Called It a Day(e)," The Road to Mandalay(e)," and "Put Your Dreams Away(e) For Another Day(e)." That year also brought eight charted singles for Little Richard, who puts his AYE up just behind his front teeth—more like AIE—so he can sing the vowel bright and dandy in songs like "Rip It Up": "got me a daite and I won't be laite! Pickin' her up in my aitey-aite." It was also the year of "Whole Lotta Shakin'," in which Jerry Lee Lewis twangs a preacher's AYE for "shakin'," "shake," and "baby." And finally, for all twenty-eight minutes of 1957's *The "Chirping" Crickets*, Buddy Holly rolls both corners of his upper lip toward his nostrils, then bounces the AYE to either his sinuses or his gullet for "that'll be the day-AY-AY" and "MAY-be BAY-by" and "uh-HAY-HAY."

Lewis was seven when "Tips" was published, Holly was six, and Richard was nine, but it's worth wondering if they ever got their hands on an old copy as kids, because their 1957 TV appearances show Sinatra's "Mouth Positions" taken to absurd places. On the *Steve Allen Show*, Lewis mugs through two entire songs, maintaining the fixed faces of "Tips" even when he isn't singing. As he vamps on the keys, Lewis stares into the camera like a blow-up doll in a curly wig, his teeth bared into the AYE-mouth and his eyes wide. Of course, a mouth this locked can't enunciate, so the lyrics barely make it out of his frozen jaw, and the line "well, we've got the bull by the horns" comes out *weehweegottaboooobahdahooorn*. Buddy Holly's mouth is smaller, a rectangle with rounded corners like a 17-inch Westinghouse set. In a December 1957 episode of *Arthur Murray Party*, he takes exaggerated pains to sing "pre-tty-pre-tty-pre-tty-pre-tty-Peg-gy-Soo-uh-oh-PAYE-ggy" as an animatronic run of all five "Tips" shapes.

Though their eccentric AYEs seem to mock vocal propriety, each singer follows a pop tradition forged by Sinatra and "Tips." In *The "Chirping" Crickets, High School Confidential*, and *Here's Little Richard*, each vocalist recorded and promoted his own "showcase vowels" to the populous. The voices of early rock, Elvis included, all gave the vowels of their lyrics an immutable stamp, and this is what Sinatra did in the 40s and 50s, with vowels that turned the crooners into balladeers. For a decade and a half, the UH of pop music was Sinatra's UH, and the AYE was his, too. *Billboard* and *Downbeat* sanctified the velvety top roundness of his AYE and the very slight "ee" he pins to any AYE on a line-break ("I did it my wAYEeeee"). These were vowels, Embassy Music Corporation said, righteous enough to be publishable.

So perhaps, when we hear Lewis, Holly, or Richard sing the motley AYEs of 1957, we hear the young singers' bids to own a vowel like real estate, to have a cartoon mouth drawn in their honor. To control the AYE, but probably for just a few years, as there are few mouths which popular music does not outgrow.

THE CARE OF THE THROAT, p 6

"Tips" insists that a popular singer's throat be swaddled and monitored like a NICU baby. Quit practicing whenever the throat feels stretched, it says, and treat even the slightest tickle with hot water, lemon, and doctors. It warns all singing bodies to "keep the feet dry and avoid sitting in a draft," though it is surprisingly tight-lipped regarding cigarettes or booze. Sinatra heeded these directives as faithfully as he did the vowel lessons in "Tips." Many of his entourage noted that he washed his hands two dozen times a day and changed his boxers at least twice on show nights. When he had his druthers (which was often), he recorded in the evening, after his throat had been given hours to loosen. And he rarely used his voice off the clock. Ava Gardner only remembers one private concert in all of their six fiery years together, when he sang her to sleep during a bumpy jeep ride across East Africa.

The prime motivator for all this throat care was fear. Sinatra's voice was legendarily fragile, as toxins, overuse, and even emotional turmoil bled all over his session tapes. Worse, sickness or stress had been known to silence him. After one strep diagnosis, he spent a week of vocal rest in an oxygen chamber, miming hand signals to his valet. And his career almost ended in 1951, when, crippled by a doomed love affair and a dirty fight over his Columbia contract, he suffered a "submucosal hemorrhage" onstage at the Copa during the most inopportune phrase of "Bali H'ai." His throat just gave: not a crack, but a mutiny that was, of course, written up in all the trades. He allegedly tried suicide that same year.

At thirty-five, smack dab in the middle of what experts call the peak of a trained baritone's years, Sinatra was slapped with a reminder: that singing is a gerrymandered bodily function. For all the research and methodology humans have applied to it, enough of singing's processes are still equal parts magic, blind faith, and— worst of all—confidence. Sinatra's voice, which Gay Talese called an "uninsurable jewel," was also an unlocatable entity that could be trained, but not trapped. Though the regions of the body most responsible for singing are easily monitored, singing itself does not calcify or clot; it cannot not be X-rayed or splinted, like our other breakable body parts. For the voice is not a body part at all.

Maybe this is what those early rockers were fighting: Sinatra's devotion to a ritual that could not be guaranteed. They pushed back at the fact that, even if a traditional pop singer followed all the edicts of vocal health and exercise, he still had to worry and pray just to keep his phantom instrument in a bankable order. To the oncoming waves of rockabillies, folkies, invading Brits, girl groups, glams, goths, new wavers, jam bands, metal heads, screamo kids, and arena rockers that followed Sinatra, this might have been a fate even more claustrophobic than the "Tips" straitjacket: that old-school squares who played by the all sonic rules could still fall prey to throat revolt.

MOUTH POSITIONS: "EE"

Fig. 3

The opening lyric of the absolutely perfect album *Frank Sinatra Sings for Only the Lonely* is "each," which he sings not with a say-cheese grin, but with lips puckered and a yawning soft palate. This makes an unusual resonant bowl under the roof of his mouth, and it gives each "each," "lonely," and "weep" on the album a jazzy bell-tone sound with a dark, blue center.

There is a fitting solitude in singing the smile out of an EE for songs like "It's a Lonesome Old Town" and "One for My Baby (and One More for the Road)." Writer Murray Kempton said Sinatra's voice "breathe[s] the loneliness of the heart," and this is what we hear in the EEs of *Only the Lonely*. They echo in his mouth as if they sit in cavernous rooms, alone with their blue thoughts. Paired with Nelson Riddle's lush arrangements, the album is by far Sinatra's most intense and artful moment: a wizened treatise on adult long-ing without a vocal seam in sight. As listeners, we revel in how a dead-sad sound can offer songs that still jazz us. Or in how, as Kempton puts it, Sinatra's singing "made us glad to be unhappy."

The only lonelier EE than *Only the Lonely*'s EE belongs to Jimmie Rodgers, "the Singing Brakeman," who often said his tips on popular singing came from boxcar tramps and fellow railroad workers. From 1927 to his death in 1933, Rodgers recorded not one, but thirteen songs called "Blue Yodel," all of them covering low-down moments from a solitary life: hard work in mean-ass towns, his decade-long struggle with tuberculosis, a lover named Thelma that deserves to be shot. He charts the pain of each "Blue Yodel" with a notched trip up the throat, from his wry tenor to the sweetest head voice this side of Vienna: *odelay-EE-eeyay-EE-oday-EE-he-hEE*.

The sonic thrill of any yodel is a vocal byproduct that Sinatra learned to mask early on: the rough "break" in the voice as it pops from chest to head. And the vowel that best showcases a break is an EE, sung with a smiling mouth, the sound placed so far back in the throat that the note clacks: "yodel-aye-EE-hoo!" Thus, Rodgers' "Blue Yodel" refrains are *Only the Lonely* turned inside out: nasal tales of the throat at work with a busy, almost baroque, finish.

And just as the sounds are divergent, so are the colors of their loneliness. Sure, both riff on the bummer of twentieth-century soli-tude, but the details of each are distant as a Hopper painting is from a Grant Wood. And their vowels are the medium for this. Up in his yodel, Rodgers amplifies the pain of failing health and life on the dole by jumping from the collective human speaking range to the EE-hurt in his worried mind. Thus, the yodel break is the hurdle a man must audibly jump in order to tell us a personal truth. It yields a skint and walloped EE, the EE of a poor man who will be dead before his thirty-sixth birthday.

Sinatra's weary pain, on the other hand, is a Beau Brummel pain.

It has health insurance. Through learned technique, he has squeezed the emotion of the vowel into a sparkling solitaire. This, then, is the loneliness of a mid-century man in his prime: forty-something, holding the world by the shorthairs, but somehow still empty in his Jack Taylor suit. Those jazzy EEs tell us that, no matter how low he gets, he'll still sleep in his warm bed tonight, then wake up and just get on with living, for as long as living may take. It's a more complicated kind of lonely, and with each EE, it brings a darker and more luxurious hurt.

"Be careful what you wish for, Joe," Sinatra's EEs warn, and then he tips us a fifty and walks out into the street.

MOUTH POSITIONS: OO

Fig. 5

Because here's the thing about EEs and AYEs and OOs: they are the atoms of song, the closest the human voice gets to the bell of a trumpet or the hole in a guitar. And if the voice that shapes them is striking enough, naked vowel lines can outrun any articulate pop lyric. Deep vowels work harder than punnery or allusion or throbbing adjectives; they don't require the brainpower of Gershwins or Leibers, or even Smokeys. Smokey Robinson, titan of "The Way You Do the Things You Do" and "Tears of a Clown," learned this firsthand in 1964, when an OO fell out of his mouth, and he knew to get the hell out its way.

He says he was onstage with the Miracles, vamping in the middle of a medley, when a particular OO melody line popped into his head "quite by accident." Sung sky-high and feathery in a *sol-fa-mi* interval, the OO was more than a hook, it was an anchor. It chained Smokey to a persona he hadn't even written yet—a lover begging OO for forgiveness and getting turned on as he grovels. He scripted that OO into the chorus of a *Billboard* Top 20 hit whose verses, though still in national airplay today, most listeners could not parrot back to you. The OO(o) line of "Ooo Baby Baby" is all they need to remember.

A year after "Ooo Baby Baby," Sinatra recorded *his* most famous OO, which, like Smokey's, was never part of any legit lyric. He is said to have hated the song in question, a limpid ballad with trite end-rhymes about a one-night stand made good. When he blew through the recording of the song in just two studio takes, he added a somewhat snide "dooby-dooby-doo" to the fade-out. This famous adlib carries a surprisingly butch OO, with none of the smitten bubbles of Smokey's. It also lacks the demureness of "Tips," which teaches that OOs need only be gentle OH-sounds with the lips "protruding slightly."

What we hear in Sinatra's "dooby" OOs is schmaltz tinged with rage; it's got to be the angriest OO in the Easy Listening catalogue. And, perhaps for that reason, it became his first number one in a decade. He performed the song for over thirty years, sometimes stopping the band to ask the crowd why they wanted to hear such a lemon for the umpteenth time. And, for a couple of those decades, his reluctant reprisal would include that scat outro, once a felt improvisation, now a stone tablet he was sick of carrying.

"Strangers in the Night" was part of his last full set, in Japan in 1994, and it fared better than other tunes on the fourteen-song bill. He still found his core pitches and clung to them, his mouth working from AYE to EE to UH like it always did. But his range was half-gone, his breath pedestrian, and all the tones of "Tips" had suffered from cell death. By his final verse, Sinatra's UH had collapsed, the AYE in "strangers" pinched, and the EEs of the song fizzled into the orchestration like afterthoughts. He did not bother to "dooby-dooby-doo."

Still, these final tours were not as deflated as many singers' last acts. The *New York Times* marveled at his "spontaneity of phrasing and intonation," and how he "still seemed compelled to experiment, trying out little tricks of phrasing, indulging in impromptu scoops and dives and interpolations that worked." He was pushing eighty and moored to a stool, but still visibly fighting, even for this song that he hated. Yes, his gaze sharpened and faded over the course of the swan songs in Japan, but when his eyes were clear, Sinatra glowered into the house, alive with the task of storytelling, straining to tell all the strangers in the Fukuoka Dome this loathsome tale of an anonymous fuck with a happy ending.

It is in this straining that we hear the one rule of "Tips" that Sinatra broke from the get-go, and continued to ignore straight through to his final vowel.

CONCLUDING REMARKS, p 32

After haughtily declaring at the end of the manual that the reader "will, undoubtedly, notice the marked improvement in [his] voice," "Tips" ends its lessons by daring the reader to pick any song "of medium range" and to sing it. If the student has followed the instructions, it says, the voice now knows what to do, so just open wide and sing "in a natural way, without straining." And this is the last tip it offers.

But *straining* is the one thing Sinatra did, without fail, from Quinlan on. Along with those iconic vowels and disappearing breaths, we always hear Sinatra straining to prove himself worthy of popular song.

We heard him, in his twenties, newly-wed and dewy, straining to summon the burdensome sorrow in "After the years / I can't bear the tears to fall / so, softly as I leave you there." And we heard him again, past forty, having sung "Softly as I Leave You" so many times that he strained to remember soft exits and what they were like three wives ago. And we heard him in between youth and middle age, singing his rudiments, drinking hot tea and checking windows for drafts, straining to prove that, no matter the song Columbia threw at him, he would dig right into its organs.

Astoundingly, nowhere in "Tips" is there a mention of understanding the songs that you sing. This shocks because, for one, it is the Quinlan lesson Sinatra remembered into his senior years. In the liner notes of his last compilation CD, Sinatra cites Quinlan not on tones or air or beans or barley, but as the man who told him "you can't sing what you don't understand." Learning this "understanding," both authors must have known, cost a hell of a lot more than than seventy-five cents. So they didn't bother mentioning it.

Only occasionally does a singer's life run dead parallel to his understanding of a song, and even then, there is a strain that shakes the music around it. With Sinatra, we only hear the direct understanding in "That's Life," in "My Way," in "Nancy with the Laughing Face," and in 1957 when, in the midst of his bust-up with Ava Gardner, he burst into the studio, took a flying leap at "I'm a Fool to Want You," and then stormed out after one five-minute take.

Unlike the strain Quinlan beat out of him in the 1930s, or that got him dropped from Columbia in the 50s, the strain to understand the constants of the American songbook while your own life and body changes is a strain that lures the populous. It is a strain that kept him relevant when many of Quinlan's other gifts left him. In the Fukuoka Dome, his entire set is a battle to sing in the face of his own decay, to spite the ossified cartridges in his larynx, his striated throat and his perforated breath.

And the old man is in luck, because pop listeners willingly concede that all voices, even great ones, must loosen and shrink. This admission is what separates the popular contract from the classical one. For us, a performer chasing down the heartbeat of a song is always welcome, as Sinatra was, to keep pushing himself. That push cannot be set upon a body like the five fixed faces of "Tips." And though the smoothness Quinlan taught young Sinatra is welcome and crucial, it is this struggle for proof that *we* strained to hear: the sixty-round live bout of Sinatra rising from the mat, sneering, and then hitting the core of our favorite songs with an open heart.

The Frontman

We were playing CBGBs. It was our first show there—sold out; we were the supporting band in like, a six-band lineup. And the night before we had crashed with friends, and of course we got fucking hammered, and I woke up running to the bathroom to puke my brains out. That was, I dunno, at seven a.m., and we weren't playing until about maybe like fourteen hours later, but the whole day I was just sick as a dog. Sick as hell.

I got to the venue, and I just stayed in the van, puking the whole time. I couldn't hold my head up; I was shaking from the intensity of my body going through it. Then one of the guys came into the van and was just like, "Yo man, we're playing." And I was like, "I'm DYING here!" and he said, "You'll be fine." We just couldn't pass this up. So I told myself, "You're fine, you're fine" and got out of the van.

At that point, I couldn't fathom the idea of pushing myself through. It's amazingly hard to be big and beefy while you're moving around the stage like I do, interacting with the crowd. These kinds of songs are so hostile and driving and quick, and I scream as hard as anyone in Metal. If I'm healthy, when I scream, I will scream through your face.

But that day, everyone was staring like, like, "He looks horrible!" I even puked in the trashcan beside the bar on my way in. When I did make it up there, somebody gave me water, and that came right back up, and I just sat on the stage, like, "Oh, no."

But we got started, I just stood up, mic in hand, and then this surge of adrenaline like I have never felt before hit me. And no shit? We played one of the best sets we've ever done, and the best ever at that venue. I mean, I floored an audience of five-to-six hundred people, and we became a staple there because of that show.

And now when I think about it, I can't believe it, especially because when you're vomiting, it rubs all over your vocal cords, and then I went and beat the shit out of my voice on top of it? But nothing bad even happened.

After the show, I just collapsed, right on stage, and laid there. Like I had punched my timecard when I was ready to work, and then when the set was over? Boom. Punched off. They dragged me backstage and put me on the toilet, and finally, like three hours later, I came to. I had no pants on. I was like, "Hey, I don't feel that bad anymore."

And what's fucked up is I've kind of never been able to top that. That's what's amazing about it, but it's also the problem. There's always going to be this struggle to find it again.

PART THREE

THE THROWN

The Interpreter

*I've heard that the telephone is a conductor of psychic
energy. When a person calls me, I ask them to say
their name three times, nice and slow. That was a
command that just came out of my mouth one day—like
instructions from the spirits to me.*

*When a client says their name, their center comes
through them into the other, so the spirits and I can find
their soul and merge with their energy. I always ask the
high self permission first, and then I begin feeling the
words of that person. And the mouth? It just works.*

*When I was first beginning, the spirits gave me a code.
I'd see a fish, and I'd tell the client, "Oh, this is what that
fish means." And I remember thinking, "Oh my God, I'm
lying!" Because I had no idea that that's what it meant.
What was happening was I heard myself saying what the
spirits were saying to the client.*

*I have noticed that the quality of my voice changes when
I channel. I go into a higher octave and my voice becomes
gentler and more soft-spoken. Unless the message that
I'm told to bring them is forceful. If the answer wants to
be amplified, I'll say, "YOU'RE NOT RECOGNIZING
THE GOODNESS WITHIN YOURSELF"—a
controlled shout! Like that.*

*I can't say what it feels like because I'm not really there
to feel it. Although when I speak to a loved one who's*

crossed over, my heart kinda bursts with their love. I begin to tear and my voice weakens from the vibrations of love that pass through me. A lot of this comes back to my chart. Mercury signifies an aptitude for communication and Scorpio allows really deep communication. There's also quite a bit of Libra in my chart. Libra energy is described as "the pleasant voice."

Please Hold

A JEAN COCTEAU ONE-ACT FROM 1930 features only a mistress and her telephone. By the end of the show, she has the black cord wrapped around her throat. "I have your voice around my neck," she whispers into the phone, her eyes perhaps bugging a bit as ominous music plays. The imaginary voice that chokes her is the soon-to-be ex-lover on the other end of her line.

She tells him, "This wire is the last thing that's joining us together," with a jokey lilt, while the audience watches her sink to the carpet, swallowing her sobs so the mouthpiece can't send them out to him. She stops crying to listen, and then says, in response to a question of his that we cannot hear, "Last night? I slept. I went to bed with the telephone." Unbeknownst to her lover, she then begins rolling around on the floor.

Cocteau was both fascinated by and wary of the telephone when he wrote *La Voix Humaine*, and he was not alone. In 1930, the in-home phone brought with it behavior that still felt foreign enough to be surreal. There were only 700,000 phones in France in 1930— party lines that wove through houses like spy periscopes, and they often forced voices to speak to each other in vague and paranoid code. Riding these phone lines, a neighborhood's voices funneled away from the neighborhood's bodies, and they reconvened, form-less, in a room built expressly for a brand new process called Public Manual Exchange.

In this room, other bodies for hire sat, waiting. They poked that bottleneck of neighborhood cords into various holes, which then connected the neighborhood voices to other, still more distant bodies. These farthest bodies held telephone receivers, and—who knows?—very well might have been thrashing about their carpeted floors.

Since the idea of loving someone with only your voice was new to Cocteau and his audience, it was worth it to sit in a theater and watch this desperate woman's one-sided conversation, if only to observe a body wearing its public voice while roiling in a private space. As Cocteau's woman wanders around her room, her gestures and expressions are dulled because her own focus stops at her neck. The rest of her somnambulates from bed to desk to wall, oblivious and vulnerable. Back then, watching an actress perform this absentminded two-step must have been like a magic trick: observe, *mesdames et messieurs*, as the voice splinters off from the body that houses it. A chick with her head cut off.

In other moments, the woman travels in the opposite direction of her voice. When she hears her lover inquire about a pair of gloves he left behind, she puts the phone down, lifts those gloves from her telephone table and kisses them "passionately." She returns to the receiver and trills, quite convincingly, that she's looked everywhere, but cannot find them. "I'll go and have another look, but I'm sure" she says calmly, all the while nuzzling the gloves with her cheek. The audience watches the lie of her words dissipate in the solitary space that is her bedroom, noting how her voice splinters from the truth of her body. *Et voilà*: A woman sawed in half.

But advertisements from that era shill phones as trusty things, like watchdogs or honest statesmen. "Sleep soundly, little lady" says one 1935 Bell magazine spread with a drowsy tot. "Mother and Daddy are near and the telephone is close by, and it doesn't go to sleep." A wordier ad from American Telephone and Telegraph announces "as the facilities for direct communication are extended, the people of our country are drawn closer together, and national welfare and contentment are promoted." But Cocteau obviously heard the telephone voice as something more discordant. The deeper this technology gets into the boudoir, he tells us, the more machines can teach us to trust things that are not true.

As the woman is hiding the gloves and the sobs from her lover, she discovers that he, too, is keeping truths out of his voice—she can hear that he is out at a place where music wafts into the mouthpiece, and not, as he claims, at home and ready for bed. When she realizes this, she does not yell gotcha, but praises him. "A lie can be useful," she whimpers into the telephone, "if you were lying to me to make the parting less painful." This is about the time she decides to choke herself with the phone cord.

Only eighty years after Cocteau's play, I am a fool if I expect any of the voices on the phone *not* to lie to me. It is part of the telephonic contract to call a help line that crackles with continental distance and hear a voice —in an accent that swirls with the music of somewhere else—introduce itself as "Brad." Often times, "Brad" will chirp "good morning!" though where he is, the sun isn't likely up. But, because I am eight decades younger than the woman in *La Voix Humaine*, I will not call "Brad" out on this lie.

And there are other voices that don't even introduce themselves, but spend all their time working to convince me that they are human at all. The cyborg voice of an 800-number asks me if I have a reservation, and when I press "1" to affirm, she comes back with a breezy, short note of praise, like a Tee Ball coach: "Great!" But when

I key in my confirmation number a little too slowly, she mutters, confused: "I'm sorry . . . didn't get that."

I try again, and she is hesitant, self-deprecating: "I *think* I understood."

I interrupt her, and she starts a bit. "—Um, could you try again?"

But after three more tries, she is miffed, and she quits me. "That is *not* a valid response. Goodbye."

Market research decided that hearing her voice, with its fibs of inflection, will soothe me. Hearing the cyborg lie about her person-hood will sweeten our time together, and make me more amenable to the human bodies that control her. It makes the distance of her voice—which goes up in outer space before it comes to me—less painful. So perhaps I am no different than Cocteau's woman, who craved to hear a vocal fib from the body she could no longer have.

What's worse, desperate little fool that I am, I tell my own lies to compensate for the fact that I'm talking to a cyborg. I change my voice to make sure she hears me exactly the way I want her to. "OTHER SERVICES," I bellow, squishing the melody of my natu-ral speech. "CAN-CEL. MY. OR-DER."

This is what phone voices are like eighty years past Cocteau—me pretending to be a robot when I am on the phone with a robot that is pretending to be like me. Sometimes, when I pace the floor of my living room, begging her to listen, I wonder if we're both speak-ing to ignore the cold fact of my phone's zero key. We share a tacit knowledge that I could press zero and make our entire relationship dissolve. But we also both know that pressing zero might just take me to some unknown voice, one as canned as hers, and that she and I have already been through so much together, so I might as well just stay on her line.

Other times, we just wait with each other on the phone—no voices, maybe some music—for long enough that my battery drains and I have to plug into the wall. She'll pop in, but when she does, her voice only guts me more: "Thank you for holding. Your call is very important. Please stay on the line." I think I can hear her sneering, a floating wet mouth with white teeth, champing at the bit for me to wrap the charger cord around myself.

The sixth time she repeats these old lines to me, I wonder, who is the woman that was once attached to this voice? How long ago did the sounds that made "your call is very important" leave her body? How did she know how "important" my call would be to her before I even made it? And where is she now? Does she ever call this line and have to talk to her old self? If so, does she upset herself as much as she is upsetting me?

And then I think of my own voice, in cans and tapes and compressed digital files, travelling around entirely independent of me, as voices do nowadays. There are thousands of occasions in which my voice has been stored out of time and place with my body. A month ago, I mailed a card that had trapped my voice singing "Happy Birthday, Baby." Last spring, my students found a YouTube clip of me onstage, and they gleefully cued the clip of me screaming onto their phones and played it when they were supposed to be peer-editing thesis statements. There is a box in my basement stuffed with tapes of me talking to myself, reciting lines in order to memorize them. And, if you telephoned me right now, because I am busy typing this, you would hear my voice from a few years ago, telling you, "Hi!"

Like most folks on the planet today, I am pushing my voice farther and farther away from myself by the hour. I try not to think about it, because if I do, I end up wondering about the moment in which our voices stop trusting *all* bodies, even the very bodies in which they originated.

The Illusionist

*When I was in undergrad, one of my directors told me
that if I didn't fix my "vocal problem," I'd never get any
work. It's hard to describe what the issue was; I have
a high and narrow upper palate, which means I don't
make K's at the roof of my mouth the way you should. I
put them way in the back, so there's a more glottal attack
and less crispness; "truck" sounds more like "truhkh."
Truly, she would get on me all the time about "that vocal
thing, that vocal thing." She still says it: "You know, you
never did fix that vocal thing."*

*By the time I got to grad school, the voice I was using was
very careful. I would over correct, slow things down, make
sure every word had the ultimate resonance, and it would
come out stilted and fake. In my first scene study class, we
were doing the Greeks, and I had an Ajax monologue—I
don't remember the play, but, you know, he's just come
back from slaughtering 250 people—and I sucked. I
truly sucked. The voice I was using was pretty much that
Richard Burton, bad college thing, sort of like AND NOW
THE HAND HATH CROSSED THE SWORD, you
know. My best attempt at James Earl Jones.*

*My classmates just looked at me like—well, actually,
they weren't looking at me; they were looking at the
ground. The instructor would say "do it again" and I
would and then he would say "stop acting with your
voice." What?*

I finally got to the point where I said, Look. If I do it the regular way I sound, it's going to come off as "Oh, look at the faggot trying to come off as a Greek hero." And that's when my classmates spoke up and said, "You have no idea. You really have no idea how we perceive you." And I said, "I guess I don't," and they said, "We think you could kick all our asses."

At this point in my life, I was six-foot-five, built like a linebacker, but that wasn't how I saw myself. I was giving that monologue feeling like an underweight soldier whose armor didn't fit. You know? The last person picked for the baseball team, the ten-year-old in the oversized sweater. So I was trying to sound like a hero—trying to create an illusion, because I didn't see myself as one. I hadn't realized yet that people with power, even if it's just physical power, they don't have to work so hard to convince people of anything. They don't have to work at all.

Double Joy: Myron Cope and the Pittsburgh Sound

I WAS DRINKING IN A TINY IOWA DIVE when I heard that Myron Cope had passed away. Actually, I didn't *hear* anything; the barmatrix had muted the television mounted above her dump-sink, so it played a silent report of the Pittsburgh sportscaster's passing. When I raised my beer-back glass in tribute, it filtered the light of the TV screen and gilded the slideshow of Myron-ic images: a tiny, Golden Cope standing slump-shouldered on the sidelines, dwarfed by Steelers. A Golden Cope grimacing on a log flume ride with Jack "Splat" Lambert. A black-and-white-and-gold photo of a headphoned Cope, smiling in the booth with a smoke and his stack of notecards. In the photos, which spanned thirty years, he is always wrinkled and bald, with wonky teeth and wild eyes. Without the sound of his voice, Cope seemed only a short man of indeterminate age who was fond of making big faces.

The TV cut to figures behind a sports news desk—men with funereal expressions who mouthed the words that coursed the bottom of our screen in robotic type. I wondered what the caption keyboard would have produced had Cope been behind the desk with those guys, for then it would have been forced to transcribe his raspy slang, like *YOI!* or *Dats alota gargonzulla!* It was also possible,

I supposed, that the captioner would detect no standard phoneme at all in Cope's legendary noise.

I turned to my friends, beer still up, and slackened my mouth to pronounce Myron's surname the same way I'd first heard it. I tried to wash the tone in that guttural Pittsburgh O: *Coehhhhhhhupe*. An O flattened by a Zamboni, the O you hear around Pittsburgh in phrases like *here we goeh* and *oehvertime* and *Francoeh Harris*, the O of the city that adopted me when I was eighteen and held me tight until I was nearly thirty.

As I saluted Cope with his own name, my bar mates, all of whom came from the very middle of America, looked puzzled. They had no idea whom I was toasting, or even if the sound coming out of my mouth was a human word. I could have responded by telling them about Cope's thirty-five seasons of color commentary for the Steelers, or his place as the first football announcer in the Radio Hall of Fame, or his sainted position as the inventor of the Terrible Towel. I should have remembered his early successes writing for *Sports Illustrated* and the *Saturday Evening Post*, when nobody doubted Cope's reporting chops, but no producer would have dared put that voice of his on air.

If Garrison Keillor has a great face for radio, Cope had a great voice for mime. In his memoir, *Double Yoi!*, Cope compares his own sound to natural disasters and violent machinery, attractive only to "two year olds and dogs." But Myron Cope was—and, four years after his death, he remains—the signature voice of Pittsburgh, a tough and goofy town with a two-faced love of both the victorious and the trodden. This might be why, that night in the Iowa bar, my first instinct was to give the patrons not a list of the man's accomplishments, but instead, a concert of his sound. Cope's voice was that of a man who spent all eighty-one years of his life smoking and yapping and spazzing out in the Allegheny Valley, and in some ways, it is all you need to know to understand my love for him. So I offered them my own weak impression, clenching into a grin I felt was not unlike the onscreen mug above us. I overworked my lips through his gravel-tongued catch phrases: *um-hah! Okel Dokel, what a dee-bacle!* and *dis is Myron Cope . . . on sports.*

When I let my faux-Cope loose, my Iowa friends looked skeptical: Nobody *really* sounds like that, do they?

I'd heard similar responses before, when I did my best "Yinzer" accent for folks who had never visited Pittsburgh. It is not an accent dramatized in TV and movies, like the sounds of Boston or Chicago or Fargo, so it's rare to hear outside the city. Plus, the most famous voices born the in Allegheny River Valley ("Mister" Fred Rodgers, Jimmy Stewart, Michael Keaton) don't really sport the dialect. You can hear a few 'Burgh tells now and again in Dennis Miller's earliest "Weekend Update" sketches, but that isn't enough to give a national presence to the noise any "Pixburgh" resident hears on public transit or at the Giant Eagle (or *Gian'iggwle*) supermarket.

It is a dialect of squarshed vowels and muddied consonants, in which the mouth alternates between working overtime and lying comically lazy. It seems obsessed with disguise; in a Pittsburgher's mouth, "ow" becomes "ah" and "ee" is sometimes "ih" and "oh" has a staticky "eh" in it. There is no "l" sound in "full," but there is one in "drawing," and there is an "r" in "wash." It makes little sonic difference if you "feel" a "steel pull" or if you "fell" into a "still pool," and "sour" sounds more like "car" than "car" does. Where I and residents of nearly a dozen states might say "y'all," they very proudly use the much rarer "yinz." And underneath all this word polka is a distinct music, one that lilts when other dialects drop and lays low when other accents ascend.

My parents drove me 750 miles from our home in Georgia to the University of Pittsburgh just a few days before freshman orientation. I remember lying, overwhelmed, in the backseat of the van as we crisscrossed the compact city for the first time. We kept falling prey to Pittsburgh's umpteen bridges and one-way streets in our searches for my dorm room, a bank, and a place to buy bedsheets. Outside the van window were dozens of geographical boundaries that stopped the town from expanding. Thirty crooked rows of roofs ran up the incline of the Monongahela's south side in layers. Their earlier citizens had run out of space on the flats, where the mills were, so they kept cramming little shotgun houses, churches, and bakeries up that huge hill, which the river had cut millennia before them. I imagined each home's secrets rolling downhill, hitting dozens of other narrow buildings before running into the water from which everyone drank.

This was a landscape so much more sedimentary than the one my parents drove back to. Back home, everything had burned in 1864, and now all the highways have at least four flat lanes per direction. In the mid 90s, when I left, Atlanta was threatening to bleed out until it met the other neutralized sprawls of the Piedmont: Charlotte, Knoxville, Birmingham, Columbia. And our accents had hemorrhaged along with that expansion, diluting the Carolina-country "I" and the Georgia red-clay "R" and the Tennessee mountain "Wh." The day my family left me in Pittsburgh, we ate in a diner by the highway entrance. My stepfather had already learned the perils of unloading his Lugoff twang on the waitstaff of Pittsburgh, so he pointed to the menu instead of ordering out loud. He looked both confused and excited when his "Pixburgh salad" arrived topped with french fries.

A few months later, I first heard Myron Cope. I was sitting on the floor of a stinky boys' dormitory, and my host had muted the Steeler game on his tiny TV and cranked WTAE on his stereo, so we could underscore the major network telecast with Cope's local radio commentary. When Cope chimed in with his color analysis, I kept having to remind myself that the radio hadn't bounced to commercial, because his voice, always cranked to a yell, was so cartoony. Bill Hargrove's calm play-by-play and Tunch Ilkin's measured analysis made Cope sound even more alien. Once I figured out that this angry puppet voice was discussing football and not trying to sell me a used Celica, minutes passed before I deciphered any words in the tattered mishmash of his speech:

> Yeah, dats da Bus *wenooanluhvt!* Indeed! *An'eesgot-uh-uh-allkinza people on'im uh-uh-like-uh-like-acennapee-dersumthinuh-uh. An'denjuss* sez I DON' CARE ABAHT DAT, you, you, *fghlieyes, thassallyarr! Anygess* up to the five yard *an'whirra'seggunangouh.*

It reminded me of the advanced French seminar I accidentally tested into that August. I dropped it not long after the first class, when the professor opened a Marseille newspaper and chatted with the rest of the group about current events. I nodded along to a conversation about either obesity or teen pregnancy—after forty-five minutes, I still couldn't tell. It was in the same class that I realized, to my horror, that my high school teachers taught me to speak French with a drawl.

What the hell does "Yoi" mean? I asked the rest of the dorm room football party, and the group died laughing. *Whut the hail!* they parroted back. *Whuuuut thuuh haaaaaail?!*

Since leaving Georgia at eighteen, I have grown obsessed with how a voice can tell me where it learned to talk. I often catch myself watching words leave people's faces to see how their sound shapes their letters into distinct speech bubbles. It's my own dorky bastardization of synesthesia, staring at spoken words as if they are tangible skins that wait for unique speech. In my mind, each human breath functions like a tire pump, the outlines of As and Es and Us hanging limp until a body breathes life into them and they float past my line of sight. As if printed words have no meaning without regional breath.

The facts of being alive push from the body, and that laced air shapes a flaccid word like "home" into the scrupulous *home* of the Corn Belt, or the double-scooped *home* of the Delta, or the grinning *home* of the Moose River Valley. And I am jealous of all these *homes*, of how a breath can exhale place along with voice, of how their speakers' rivers are their skin and the hills are their bones, and their lives are places that speak in unison with their languages.

In the lateral Os of speakers like Cope, I hear the hills of Pittsburgh's east side, where many Lithuanians made their homes a hundred years ago. Cope grew up a few blocks from the high school where Fred and Gene Kelly taught dancing for a quarter and a quick bus trip to the college from which we both graduated, and that's a part of his *home*, too. And I hear the fence made by the Monongahela three miles to the south, the Allegheny 3.4 miles north, and the Ohio five miles out his back door.

William Labov calls the Pittsburgh sound "the Galapagos Island of American dialects" and blames it on the factories that, in the Industrial Revolution, dumped dozens of cultures into the valley cavity. Irish verb forms and Yiddish vocabulary and Slavic vowel changes were reined in by the hills, and these sounds met and mutated in the riverfront markets. And while this collision took place, Pittsburgh's topography kept the sound from spreading, and it prevented sonic infiltration from the neighbors in Ohio or Eastern Pennsylvania. Once their sounds had evolved into the least likely of speech patterns, residents united to fight the regional flattening that ran rampant through the Mid-Atlantic from the First World War onward. For one hundred years, Pittsburghers forced Pittsburghese to clot.

You hear the smorgasbord of tones and words in many of Cope's catchphrases, which he unleashed into the air with dizzy vigor. His *dumkoff*—used to describe a foolish play or any dissenting opinion—is garbled German, while the mighty *Yoi!* is either Eastern European or Yiddish, depending on who you talk to. *Yonko*, which roughly means a babbling bore (and what Cope renamed Denver's football team in 1977) is most closely related to something in Russian. And *yinz* is a reinterpretation of an Ulster-Scots second-person-plural that floated up from Appalachia, where Cope's wife, the famous-but-faceless Mildred, was born.

A staunch linguist would want me to note that most of the major aspects of Cope's sound do exist in other accents across this continent, which means Pittsburghese is not as unique as all the Yinzer-themed T-shirts and coffee mugs and Cope fans would have us believe. Still, they should concede that this dialect has very little in common with the dialects of its closest neighbors, which makes it seem impenetrable and stubborn. Pittsburghese barely overlaps, if at all, with the vowel sounds of Cleveland, a town not three hours from Heinz Field. And Cope writes about how attracted he was to Mildred's exotic drawl, even though she grew up not ninety miles south of where he did.

What's more, many of these same linguists will admit that the particular *grouping* of these odd vowels and vocal changes does produce an anomalous noise, especially for an outsider to experience. Nowhere did the raw materials of the voice end up in such a tizzy as they did in the 'Burgh. Many older Pittsburgh residents can attest to this, noting that the first time they even *knew* they had an accent was when they travelled over Mount Washington, or hosted an out-of-town guest who wrinkled their noses and said, "you talk funny."

My freshman-year friends were all from Western Pennsylvania, and the whole semester, they giggled through bad impressions of how I talked. Usually this involved devoting twenty seconds to each word or syllable I spoke. One of my angry retorts, *Fuuck y'awl; fuuuck awwl y'awwwl* became their catchphrase, which they screamed into the crowd at Pitt stadium and into the fountain at Point State Park. Until that fall, I had never considered myself someone with a particular way of talking.

Still, it was a fun and wordy first season away from home, especially when I got to spend a weekend off-campus, with friends who brought me and my laundry to meet the parents. Often, I was shocked to see the names of their satellite towns spelled out on road signs, as they had been pronounced so differently back at the dorm: Duquesne, Versailles, Sewickley, Blawnox. At the dinner table, the moms would smirk when I stressed the first syllable in TV or used only one syllable for the words "towel" and "oil." I remember having to pay extra close attention the deeper I got into Pittsburgh life. Families spoke so quickly, and with a vocal shorthand much more difficult to keep straight than the ways Pittsburgh kids talked in class. When somebody's dad asked me *you dunno what yer major is yet*, the singsong underneath his words peaked at "major" and then slid down in pitch. After "yet," I waited for him to say something else, then realized that these people's questions had no question marks.

But by the time the Steelers beat the Panthers in the last game of the 1996 regular season, either my friends had stopped noticing my accent, or it stopped being noticeable. By sophomore year, when Myron Cope had nicknamed the Steelers' new quarterback "Slash," I had begun noticing how slowly my stepfather spoke when he called me on the phone.

In *Double Yoi!*, Cope tells of how WTAE, the station that hosted his first call-in show, once imported a new station manager from Los Angeles. At the end of his first day, the Suit had written "fire Myron Cope" on a legal pad as his first order of business. "He had . . . reacted much as do strangers motoring through the Pittsburgh area," Cope writes. "Hearing my voice assault their eardrums for the first time, they exclaim, 'What *is* that?'" Other WTAE executives dissuaded the Suit, probably stressing that this is how Pittsburghers prefer to be talked to, thank you very much.

When Cope was designing that now-famous radio show, he planned a program that would "replicate the evenings I had spent as a teenager idling with pals on a street corner in front of Sol's Pharmacy," where local kids fought about sports "until a familiar red-faced cop arrived in a patrol car and ordered us to disperse." The pull of Cope rests heavily on this street-corner conviviality, which he maintained as the sports world developed a more neutral national polish. On the air, he sounded like an excitable kid from the old neighborhood, even when the broadcast voices around him were much more buffed-out. "Listeners," he writes, "became—how should I put it?—inured to my voice. Not enraptured, but inured." Because nothing says Pittsburgh like a relationship born from a good, stiff toughening up.

That voice also garnered fans because it reconstructed a Pittsburgh that was already ceasing to exist. There was no Sol's Pharmacy by 1973, and who knows what had happened to Cope's red-faced cop. But folks in that town are haunted by what's no longer there. Ask a lifer for directions and they'll tell you to turn left *where da ol' Sinclair station useta' be* or to pass *'at schoow 'at burnt dahn a few years ago.* Perhaps this is something to be expected from a town whose past became the past quite rapidly, as millions of residents flooded outward with the closings of the mills in the 80s and 90s. Then, hundreds of thousands immigrated in the new century, when the city switched its focus to tech and medicine, altering the timbre of Pittsburgh even further.

But although Sol's and the mills were gone, Cope was still on the air for those die-hard Pittsburghers, and he sounded exactly like he did back on the corner. Cope's callused voice confirmed his ethos not just as the spokes-sound of football in the Rust Belt, but as what it meant to be a Pittsburgh fan from all the way back, when the belt was much rustier. Cope never wanted to become a national voice; he often claimed he never even wanted to be on the radio. He says he just planned to *yoi* and *double yoi* until his luck ran out, and it just never did. When the Steelers (finally) started winning titles, that voice was a half-octave deeper and considerably more tobacco-stained, but his listeners still said *doehn't change a thing*.

I suppose I see the fade-out of my own accent as a sad contrast to Myron Cope, who, in the face of professional ridicule, not only kept his dialect, but turned it into a bankable trademark. Few Americans today can say they speak with the same music as their fathers, or even with that of their younger selves. I cannot tell you what my voice sounded like when I was yukking it up on the sidewalks of Gwinnett County (though I'm sure the conversation topics were much stupider than pro sports). I do know that, as an adult, I sound enough like the rest of the world to erase any curiosity about my origins. I've lost that street-corner voice, along with my street corner.

What's worse, I've magpied a few random changes from my nomadic adulthood, and now my accent sounds at best misguided, and at worst insane. I sometimes roll my Os in "obviously" like an Iowan, or snap my As in "Grand Rapids" like a West Michigander. Thanks to nine years in the 'Burgh, my diphthong in "down" still sags a bit, and I use the word "jagoff." And Lord knows what I've picked up from the TV.

According to Pittsburgh linguist Barbara Johnstone, versions of my plight happen to most Americans from Generation X onward. She blames better access to a world of recorded voices, easy transportation, and white-collar jobs requiring "strong communications skills" for the waning of regional sound. This loss deepens the more a person puts herself out into the world and the less isolated her home becomes. And it's a double-edged sword, according to Johnstone. The more a person moves around the country (either physically or virtually), the more her accent will fade, but only in leaving her hometown will she discover she has an accent she wants to retain. Dialect awareness is complacent with dialect loss, Johnstone says. And often, once they become aware of the sounds of their past, homesick expats scurry to preserve them.

This is a very loose explanation of the linguistic concept of "enregisterment," in which a group legitimizes—and in some cases, even scripts—a dialect in order to keep the local identity alive in the face of globalization. One hundred years ago, Johnstone notes, Pittsburgh papers talked about their speech in pejorative contexts—as "nasal" farm talk that "gives the distinct impression of ignorance." But by the time a "folk dictionary" called *How to Speak Like a Pittsburgher* was published in the early 80s, Pittsburghese was a winsome sound, a sound of membership in the Pittsburgh club. And, it must be noted, this was now the club of Cope and of the Steelers, who had just won four Superbowl rings in six years.

Enregisterment happens, Johnstone says, when "people become aware that they don't talk like their grandparents, and that their kids don't have the same accent they do. They think 'wait a minute; maybe we should preserve some of it.'" But, she notes, this preservation does not come in the form of enforcing Pittsburghese in the home, or signing their kids up for private Yinzer lessons; it comes in the form of Pixburgh-themed T-shirts and coffee mugs, in novelty manuals and in dolls like Chipped Ham Sam, a mulleted poppet that, when you squeeze him, says *Djinzeet yet? Ahm gettin' hungry fer uh sammich.*

"That's bizarre!" Johnstone said when describing Sam to a lecture crowd in 2007. "You don't find that kind of thing in other cities. Just the fact that their speech is *so* important." This importance, as I see it, runs right alongside the famed run of Cope's broken voice. Cope *was* the Pittsburghese that did not defect when his town smoothed itself out, and his tenure was the groundwork that made sound—not architecture or food or handiwork, but *sound*—Pittsburgh's touchtone to the past. Maybe they held onto that broken sound because they knew that the rest of Pittsburgh was going to get fixed, but their hearts would still want for broken things. If so, the Yinzer purists were much smarter than I was, or than most of us American English speakers were. And they were doubly wise for choosing Cope as their commemorative instrument.

At this point, it seems a given that Myron Cope fuels Pittsburghese enregisterment. The steadfast music in Cope's voice proved something to his friends, acquaintances, and listeners, especially those that lived far away and felt they had lost their town. Cope's voice, dried up by scotch and stogies (and later, throat cancer), *sounded* like Pittsburgh looks and feels: a glorious place of hard-bitten landscape and anomalous energy—a town with a team that couldn't win a game for decades and then rallied to win them all.

But his trump card came not in ugliness, but in joy. Cope's sound was a happy-ending narrative of hard knocks that led to a heyday, because each ripped-to-shit phoneme was paired with his noted joviality. *Yoi!* and *double yoi!* and—on rare occasions that thousands remember—*almost quadruple yoi!* amplified their world with a boyish explosiveness. His haggard cheers launched from their radio speakers like pumice exclamation points.

And now, sitting at a keyboard in a town in which I haven't heard any kind of accent for weeks, it all makes sense. What better way to broadcast the heart of Pittsburgh than with the sound of a raspy, self-made spaz, just shy of five feet five inches tall? There, in Cope's smoky cords and stunted growth plates, listeners could experience the noise of their city, not necessarily as it was, but as how they liked to remember it. Piped through his chest, teeth, and cheeks were horns, exhaust, trolley cars, bar gibber, and the sound of a river so full of work that it occasionally caught fire. Listeners turned up their radios, took a deep breath and sighed, no matter where they lived: *'Derz noe place like hoehme.*

The Illustrator

Well. This is some show, I'll tell ya. And now, the Bears in a seemingly impossible situation—they have only one time-out left, they pretty well have to run it back to save the game and boy, talk about a heartbreaking way to lose.... It's unlikely that Ford can get the ball and get out of bounds far enough upfield to set up one try at the field goal.

Alright here we go with the kickoff. Harmon will probably try to squib it—and he does. Ball comes loose. The Bears have to get out of bounds. Rogers along the sideline, another one—they're still in deep trouble at midfield, they tried to do a couple of—the BALL IS STILL LOOSE as they get it to Rogers. They get it back now to the 30, they're down to the 20—OH THE BAND IS OUT ON THE FIELD!—He's gonna go into the end zone! He got into the end zone!

Will it count? The Bears have scored! But the bands are out on the field! There were flags all over the place! Wait and see what happens; we don't know who won the game; there are flags on the field. We have to see whether or not the flags are against Stanford or Cal. The Bears may have made some illegal laterals; it could be that it won't count.

The Bears, believe it or not, took it all the way into the end zone. If the penalty is against Stanford, California

*would win the game. If it is not, the game is over
and Stanford has won. We've heard no decision yet.
Everybody is milling around on the—FIELD! And the
BEARS! THE BEARS HAVE WON! THE BEARS
HAVE WON! OOOhmyGOD!*

*The most amazing! Sensational! Dramatic! Heart
rending, exciting, thrilling, finish in the history of college
football! California! Has Won! The Big! Game! Over
Stanford!*

*Oh, excuse me for my voice, but I have never, never seen
anything like it in the history of I have ever seen any
game in my life! The Bears have won it! THERE WILL
BE NO EXTRA POINT.*

Playing Sick

> Ultimately the basis for all disgust is *us*—that we live and die and
> that the process is a messy one emitting substances and odors
> that make us doubt ourselves and fear our neighbors.
> —William Ian Miller

THE MOST BASIC TRIGGER TO THAT WHICH REVOLTS us is a
hard-wired recognition of what we cannot abide in our mouths. The
unsavory, the revolting, the rotten. Across cultures, human disgust
dials directly back to this simple rejection: we open our mouths
and spit. It's a frank distinction between the mouth—soft, vulnerable gateway to our organs and viscera—and the countless foreign
bodies that might try to enter it. And while biology compels us to
eject offensive objects from our mouths, we are not compelled, at
least initially, to voice this ejection. Primal disgust happens without
speech or internal monologue. Our two vocal cords stay still and
separate as the tongue rolls out or reels back.

> *(Like waking up one morning and groggily feeling a*
> *bug crawl across my cheek and toward my mouth.*
> *Knowing, as I jerked into consciousness, if I opened*

*my lips to say anything, I'd taste its filthy, evil legs
on my tongue).*

But when small boys dare each other to poke worms that writhe in
gutter puddles, they exhale sound as they inch toward the worm's
segmented body. Their necks retract. Their teeth chomp forward,
fencing in the mouth-hole: "*Ee*." Then, lips encircle teeth, puckering
like drawstring hoods: "w." This is the literal vocabulary of slamming
the door between our sensitive tissue and a world of offenses. In
this word "*Eew*," they show that they don't need to put the worm in
their mouth to know that it tastes disgusting. And up through the
windpipe to meet this face: a tone in head-voice.

> *(But not like when, at the cast party of my first big
> acting job several years ago, I grabbed the wrong
> open Coke bottle and drank a watery mess of
> discarded cigarette butts, spitting it back before my
> tongue could push it toward my throat.*
>
> *I don't remember how it tasted; all I feel when I
> recall the moment is a rolling, nauseous shame. The
> fear that someone saw me, dolled up and nervous
> to be there, making such an asinine mistake. The
> spit was silent, but, back past my throat and into my
> body, it was, somehow, voiced.)*

When people ask me what part of theater I find the most challeng-
ing—crying, kissing, being naked onstage, remembering all those
lines—I usually answer "making people laugh." Not that I find any
of these other tasks easy, but they are all, at least, rehearseable.
Ninety percent of my work is in comedies, which introduce a terrifying variable into the mix every night. While delivering a play-

wright's jokes, the actors must make room for the sound of the crowd, changing their play as the laughs arrive in different places, for different lengths of time, and at different intensities. Playing for laughs is a balancing act; you have to both acknowledge the audience's laughter and completely ignore it. Become too aware of the audience or the litany of jokes the script forces you to shoot at them, and you're sunk.

In every show, I manage to find a seemingly innocuous line, or bit, or piece of business that I cannot figure out. The frustration makes me abandon the audience each time I try the joke. And then I muck through it alone, night after night, tuning out the house while wriggling in my own self-disgust.

The seventh line of the play is "Eew," and, though it's not a line you see in lots of scripts, I can't remember the first time I delivered it, at the audition. Pages in hand, pretending to feel at home on an invisible set that wouldn't be built for months, I was preoccupied with the weird task of convincing a director that I belonged in his speculative concept, which he called "the world of the play." I was far too focused on this to plan the perfect delivery of an unusual line like "Eew." My only concern was to have "Eew" blend in and not stop the flow of my audition. It appears to have not, as I ended up with the role.

Once I'd been hired to play Mimi the waitress, I began working through the script and noticed that "Eew" appears again and again in her dialogue. I saw that I'd be saying "Eew" five times a night, in response to five different lines in the fifty-five-page script, convincing first my director and then a paying crowd that five separate concepts grossed me out.

> CLAUDE: Fricasseed platypus, stuffed with turnips,
>   served on a bed of sautéed Argentine
>   grasshoppers.

(Mimi makes a sound of disgust)

MIMI: Eew.

Disgust expert Paul Rozin notes that North Americans like myself can split the things that disgust us into nine categories. Food. Death and dying. Emissions and fluids of the body. Animals. Sexual activities. Corpses. Unnatural entrances through the flesh "envelope." Interpersonal contact with humans who are either hygienically or morally contaminated.

Rozin adds that certain elicitors can disgust us for more than one categorical reason. Filthy animals, like slugs and worms, might also disgust because they resemble our own bodily fluids and waste, or because of their similarities to the unreliable tongues that police the fragile envelopes of our mouths. Vultures disgust us both because they eat contaminated flesh and because we know that one day we, too, could be vulture food. Those with a heightened sensitivity to disgust, Rozin notes, usually also harbor an amplified fear of death. Mimi the waitress's "Eew"s are spoken in reaction to a series of images that hit various categories on Rozin's list:

- eating grasshoppers (p. 10: animal)
- viewing photos of a corpse (p. 21: corporeal)
- the bones of a starving man poking through his flesh (p. 22: envelope violation)
- shoving paté down a bunny's throat (p. 28: envelope/animal), and
- Ernest Hemingway meeting the business end of a shotgun one night in Idaho in 1961 (p. 49: corporeal/envelope/fear of death and dying).

I often see punch lines as music rather than language. If I can identify the pitch, tone, and timbre of the character I've been cast to play, I'd just as well sing the line rather than act it. I count sentential rhythms meticulously, scouring lines for repetition, especially threes, or for sounds with vowels that can be stretched or clipped or yodeled out. This is a trick that nearly always works. So I must have first tried to see that "Eew" as a musical note—not an "Eew," but, rather, an out-of-tune E-flat.

One night, early on, I spoke Mimi's lines to my empty apartment, and all five "Eew"s hit false notes. Even though I felt my face instinctively prepare for the sound of "eew"—scrunching and wincing, neck jerking back a little as I must have at some disgusting point in my own life—the actual sound of the word felt foreign and ridiculous. I tried the line in a series of vocal poses: "Eew" *(at full volume).* "Eew" *(soft and plaintive).* "Eew" *(descending tones).* "Eew" *(low-to-high).* "Eew" *(eyes wide).* "Eew" *(eyes slits).* "Eew" *(brows knitted).* "Eew" *(face neutral).* This wore the word out the first day I owned it. While trying to grimace and pitch my way into its intent, I squeezed its meaning until it hung, limp and desiccated, in my throat. Without the spontaneity of a surprising, disgusting event, I couldn't get it to make any sense in my mouth.

I wondered how it was that a word I'd said scores of times in my life seemed so impossible to conjure in the persona of this French waitress. I began jotting down every "Eew" I heard in its natural habitat:

- *Monday 7/18*: Upon learning that my friend, a new mother, had leaky breasts.
- *Thursday, 6/5*: Hearing how a friend's idiot paramour had text-messaged her while he was in bed with another woman.
- *Friday, 6/22*: Watching my cat vomit.
- *Monday, 7/9*: Looking at the filthy fingernails of a cast member that I had to touch.

The natural-born "Eews" would shoot from my mouth, perfectly formed, before I could catch them, fueled by a belly-lurch in the rhythm of each two-way conversation. I tried to rewind them, relying on my short-term memory to reconstruct the "Eew" in perfect pixels. No luck.

There were also unvoiced moments where I *felt* as revolted as Mimi might when she envisions eating grasshoppers or looking at the corpse of a Nobel Prize-winning writer, but no sound came out of my face. I'd feel a Mimi-style shudder in my throat as my stomach stopped short, and then nothing. All these silent reactions happened when I was alone:

- Replaying a barroom argument where I talked a little too much trash.
- Passing a mirror while not wearing a shirt.
- Washing dishes that I'd left sitting for a deplorable amount of time.

So a voiced "Eew," it appeared, was a public act, a socially normed self-report of my body encountering stimuli within earshot of another living thing. Even in natural speech, it seems, an "Eew" is a performance of sorts. Then does this mean that even everyday "Eews" are forced? And what kind of disgust is the mute feeling that takes me when no one else is around?

> (*Like the art book on my shelves that with the picture of that motorcycle crash victim. Belly-down on a tin gurney, he's missing the lower half of his face. What's there is an almost cartoon-shaped explosion of skin, unframed by lips or jawbone, just red and pink, string and sinew, hanging down like willow*

branches. Above the mess, a bald head, blue eyes, eyelashes clumped with wet.

Just passing that book and knowing the image is between its bindings makes me shudder. Remembering the fat, dripping tongue, lolling past the flesh and into the gauze on the gurney).

In 1971, a team of researchers at the Children's Hospital of Pittsburgh invented the "Mister Yuk" sticker in response to fears that the current symbol for poison, a skull-and crossbones, might symbolize adventure to children rather than toxicity (especially in the hometown of the 1971 World Series Champion Pirates). Mister Yuk is an asparagus-green circle-head. Painted across his face are black diagonal eyes and brows, a convex mouth, and a vertical, oblong tongue. He makes the same instructive face a mother might when she catches her infant licking a penny. Though frozen, this is a violent and active response, one usually voiced with a cartoonish retching. The sound is a contradiction, hocking up and shutting off at the same time; the hollowness of the open vowel thinned by the closed throat. In English, we've gone so far as to spell this face: *yuck.* Vocabularized spit.

Thus, the name, the word, the sound, the face are all lessons, prompting both physical and internal responses from their young audiences. They grab each developing lexicon by the chin and force each mouth to gape, then expectorate. We see precursors to Mister Yuk's frozen face in Noh theater or in the hands and bodies of centuries-old Hindu texts. In these images, it becomes obvious that only a few broad strokes are needed to tell any audience that an object is gross. If only, I thought, instead of trying to sell this wretched "Eew," I could turn my face green, my features *trompe l'oeil.* Disgust seems to play much better in two dimensions than in one.

So I watched clips of the cartoonish Lucille Ball, with her own classic (and nearly Classical) gesture and noise for "Eew." Lucy sells the sound as a compartmentalized comedy bit, a one-two-three punch spelled differently than Mimi's, possibly "uhEEEwww." We've seen her make this face in a variety of situations: inadvertently eating snails, dipping her feet into a vat of grapes, downing a spoonful of Vitameatavegamin.

The first step of her sound is a prologue: she directs all of her energy and posture to the thing that will disgust her—the waiter explaining how *escargot* translates, for example. Mouth slack, body twisted into an obscuring profile, eyes boring into her scene partner, she waits, appearing almost hungry for the offensive information. Upon the utterance of the disgusting line, Lucy lets the energy of his word slap her like a violent hand. Next, she reels away from him, howls (the vowel is "uh," due to the slack mouth) and swings her body toward the audience, morphing her face as she swivels. The teeth clench, the eyes squint, and the mouth widens into an oblong grimace.

Once she faces full front, her howl rises in pitch and the mouth stretches 'uh" into "eee," leaving her chest and moving up into her nose. Then, finally, as coda, the sound descends back to her chest as she freezes in a more relaxed, but still grimacing, frown. This is the mug she holds for laughs. She performs reaction in at least a dozen episodes without wavering from the formula at all, as if it were spliced in during postproduction with anachronistic camera patchwork. Like most parts of comedy, it's too technically perfect to be spontaneous, more like a dance move than a moment of vérité. But it sells because *something* in it is not false. She somehow, in all of her flat, Apollonian exactness, gives it the heightened energy of a real recoil. A parody of the face we saw our mothers make. Of course "uhEEEwww" also "works" in the comedic scene because it sounds funny, especially with Lucy's nasal delivery, which she uses for other catch phrases, both linguistic ("Ooo Rickeeeee!") and nonlinguistic ("Waaaaaaaaah!").

I tried Lucy's "uhEEEwww" in rehearsals, revving up, swinging full front, mugging in the afterglow. The result felt like pulling the E-brake on a moving train. It was too long and involved for one character to perform in the presence of five others. It also wasn't my bit to land. I don't know what I was thinking, offering such an operatic take on such an insignificant line. The play is not, after all, called *I Love Mimi*, and the show's arc is not to set her up for an aria of punch lines. At the moment of the above "Eew," for instance, all the other actors had been blocked with their backs to me; they were busy with the actual plot. The saddest mugging happens when one mugs alone.

My director reminded me how the line was spelled in the script. With only two letters and one-and-a-half phonemes, there's no way to fit a three-step Lucy-style "uhEEEwww" aria into "Eew." Maybe the playwright's spelling of a double-e "eew" (instead of Webster's "ew") indicates lighter touch, more wrinkled nose than grotesque grimace. Like an "Eeek! A mouse!" I tried cutting Lucy's three-part mug off at both ends, axing the "uuuu" and the "www," the soprano midpoint "eeee" remaining. It sounded like I was singing the theme from *Psycho*.

> (*Like the pinfish I caught, standing alone on a sea wall when the rest of my family had gone into the condo to take naps. Shocked that something actually bit my line, I stared at the hook in its jawing mouth, piercing the pink tissue right where its tongue would be.*
>
> *I heard bones cracking before I touched it. EEEEEEEEEEEEEEEEEEEEEEEE it said.*

> *So I bashed it against the side of a wall until it*
> *stopped moving).*

Mister Yuk's crayon face and Lucy's loud punim both mirror Charles Darwin's work a century earlier in *Expression of the Emotions in Man and Animals.* Chapter Eleven's illustration plate shows model Oscar Rejlander performing a dead-on Mister Yuk: eyes dark, nose and eyebrows straining as if they might touch, tongue unraveled into the beard. "The protrusion of the tongue in letting a nasty object fall out of the mouth," Darwin says, "may explain how it is that lolling the tongue universally serves as a sign of contempt and hatred."

Yet when lovers pair off, huddle in a quiet corner, and shut their eyes, they *enjoy* making that Mister Yuk face, or Rejlander's face, into each other's open mouths. The fervent Yuk. The exploratory Yuk. And, further, a modified "yuck" response as well. Eyes squeezed shut, the tongue relaxes and uncoils, as it would were it tasting bile, but then it pulls backward and beckons instead. Like the mouth has changed its mind and decided that, rather than spitting its lover out, it wants him back inside. So it sends its own tongue to tell the other tongue, *come hither.*

Here, disgust pulls a *Freaky Friday* and channels intimacy, or at least want. Desire suspends fear. Tongues, soft arbiters of genes and disease, are forgiven their trespasses. The lover allows the tumescence of the muscle, its porous top, and smooth, cordoned underbelly, and all the warm live cultures floating around it. A ready mouth will take all this in, not as foul medicine, but as sugary tonic. After each stab of the tongue, the mouths close in on one another, demurring into twin puckers. Bee-stung mouths pantomiming "Eew" in unison.

Darwin found *Expressions of the Emotions in Man and Animals* one of his most difficult books to write. He and two of his children spent the Spring of 1872 knee-deep in convoluted proofs, photographs, and questionnaires, trying to communicate the connection between language, gesture, emotion, and our primal ideas. Unable to untangle the messy and inconclusive draft, he confessed to a friend that the process made him "sick of the subject, and myself, and the world." How far must that learned disgust have felt from a simple worm in the mouth.

According to Paul Rozin, somewhere in the past few thousand years, disgust has evolved. We've taken the feeling behind spitting out poison and connected it to other behavior. We use it to judge the animals ("They are an abomination to you, and you detest them. You shall not eat of their flesh and you shall detest their carcasses") as well as the actions of other humans ("Stop picking your nose, you filthy boy!"). Even more recent is a disgust that recognizes moral or spiritual filth ("Pervert. You disgust me"). In that version, disgust is an attack, an interpersonal shaming device.

Rozin and his team spent much of the 1990s asking citizens from dozens of cultures to list what disgusted them. It turns out that moral offenses far outnumber physical ones these days. The most universally disgusting thing, according to Rozin's research, is not ingesting feces or sharing a bowl with a dog, but donning a sweater once worn by Hitler. Here, Rozin says, the mouth expresses in those words, sounds, and faces an intent not to guard the physical body, but, instead, to guard the soul.

We also now use it to look inside ourselves and get grossed out. We can stand in judgment of our own rottenness and say "yuck" in rejection of our actions, or our thoughts. We can swallow Yuk, digest him and use him for fuel. Like Darwin did that spring, trapped in a project, a performance at which he felt he'd never succeed.

> *("Like, just say it," a young actor told me a few days before we went into tech rehearsal. "You're totally*

> *stuck in your head. Just stop analyzing yourself open*
> *your mouth: Eew. See?")*

Halfway through our three-week run, there was a night when I was tired. We'd done two shows already that weekend and my shoes pinched. I was midway through a closed-mouthed yawn when I heard one of the cue lines and, terrified of the silence, I just spat the damn word. It was a short sound, some alto tone too brief to register. I imagined half a wavelength hitting the lip of the stage and then skipping across the house like a glossy stone. The audience howled. Two actors turned to me as they held for the laugh, their eyes twinkling.

Of course, the following afternoon, at the Sunday matinee, I tried it again and the audience barely stopped opening their wrapped candies. I said the next lines on autopilot while scolding myself on the inside. *Yeeeeeeech. You stupid fucking idiot.*

Three years ago, Rozin amended his internationally recognized Disgust Scale, adding the very latest in disgust to his list: "magical thinking." Rozin's twenty-first-century subjects report that they are most disgusted by 100 percent pure pieces of chocolate fashioned to resemble dog turds. They say they would never eat soup that had been stirred by a flyswatter, even if the flyswatter was obviously new or if they'd seen it sterilized. Apparently, millennial disgust has moved past edibles and even past moral codes. We humans can now use our imaginations to disgust ourselves past the bounds of logic.

Like how, the minute you begin to doubt your ability to deliver a harmless little white line, it becomes illogical. You find yourself anticipating it and dreading the way your gut will feel after it's been said. A doubted line becomes a personal cliché. Meaningless, like "to be or not to be." Impossible, like "You talkin' to *me*?"

This, for me, is where disgust truly meets performance—in the magical, transformative power of doubt. Once it starts, it's there for-ever, reminding you of just how unnatural your job really is. *Look at you*, it says, as you stand in a pinned-together skirt and spray-painted shoes, pretending that the doors that keep you onstage can actually lock and that the hundreds of people in front of you aren't visible. *Who in heaven's name do you think you are?*

You unpack all the fairy dust that allows you to "be" another per-son—the careful orchestration of lights, the snappy patter, and the powder—and the self is all you're left with up there. It is a terrible thing when you forget the lightness of pretending, the grace and the delicacy of comedy, and snap yourself into reality, in which you are burdened by this exposed and doubting self. It is a soft self that feels almost liquid and bloody, a bad self, shoved into view against its will.

You grasp the plywood flats of the set pieces, dig your fingers into the reupholstered divan, trying to hold onto something external that will take that self and shove it back down your throat. Because that is a self is not supposed to be here. Because that self is revolting.

The Shape-Shifter

There's this whole subculture of guys like me who provide impressions as "sound-alikes" for movie trailers or TV. So, when they're editing a Jack Nicholson movie for TV and they can't have him saying "motherfucker," they'll hire me to do Jack saying "monkeyfeather"—which is an even better swear word. But you can't pay Jack Nicholson enough to say "monkeyfeather."

My mom is an actress, so growing up, I was always around people that could do accents and dialects and who played their voices like an instrument. For fun, I would try to imitate them. I would watch impressionists like Rich Little or Frank Gorshen, and it was just galvanizing to watch them zip around. For a person who's self-defensive, as most children are, it was a cloak: "I can be invisible whenever I want." That's what impressions do for me. I disappear for a second and this other guy shows up, and it's not a mental illness because I can control it.

Now, after I've done this for years, there's a link between the recording of the voices that I have in my mind and the physicality of my vocal equipment. There are these threads—it's probably electronic—that string from my mind file just as fast as the decision to do Jack Nicholson. I don't have to take the time to do anything. It manifests itself physically and sonically. I don't consciously move my throat, lips and tongue; I just find myself doing it. It's like a little mind app.

But this one time, it was kind of weird. I've been doing that Shakespeare bit in my one-man shows for twenty years where I'll have an audience member pick voices from this list of seventy-five and then I'll do Clarence's dream from Richard III. *One night during my one-man show, somebody called out "John Gielgud!"*

Now, I had grown up listening to recordings of Gielgud and I would always make my mother laugh doing Gielgud, so I'd been doing him for fifteen to twenty years without ever really flubbing, but this one night, I couldn't find it. I just—I corpsed. And I found out later John Gilegud *had died that day. I don't even want to try to explain the metaphysical implications of that.*

Overall, I think impressions resonate with people because of a fundamental interest that we all have in identity. Identity is one of these really deep questions; we're always asking, "Who the hell am I?" So I think it's very therapeutic for people to watch another person juggle two, three, or more identities. Because, the truth is, lots of us feel locked into the one.

A Monstrous Little Voice
(with T. Foley)

Tuesday, November 15, 2011

Dear **HECTOR**:

We would like to congratulate you on making the significant (and brave!) decision to uncover your REAL voice, and also to thank you for soliciting our Voice Discovery Service Package. What follows is our storied method, guaranteed to match ventriloquist dummies with just-right independent voices so that they can live more fulfilling lives "off the knee."

Automaton no more; you're now on your way to autonomy!

HECTOR, we understand that finding your own voice can be a daunting task, especially for those dummies who have been "spoken-through" for decades-long careers. We also understand that discovering your voice is an emotional journey, one that can leave you with many doubts. Some questions cycling through your head right now might include:

- *Will my jokes still be funny in my new voice?*
- *How will I know how to "work" my voice? Will I need to take a training course, like Toastmasters?*
- *Will my new voice get me more dates, both professional and romantic?*
- *What if my new voice gives me seizures, like that lady's from* Entertainment Tonight *did to her biggest fan?*

We implore you, however, to push those thoughts from your mind, as they will all be addressed at the appropriate juncture. The first step of this exciting process is simply admitting that you *have* a voice . . . or, at least, that you *deserve* one. Do you feel prepared to do that, **HECTOR**? Can you let yourself have a voice of your own?

Good. Then you're ready to begin.

Now is where we take over, with our PATENTED QUESTIONNAIRE that is GUARANTEED to pinpoint not just the *type* of voice that suits you best, but the myriad little details (rasp, resonance, dialect) that will make your new voice the unique snowflake it deserves to be. Then, all you have to do is pick the voice from our catalogue, pay a fee for installation, and you'll be "in good voice" forever (as long as you refrain from smoking, cheerleading, careless karaoke, and extensive work with harsh industrial chemicals)!

Okay, **HECTOR**: Are you ready? LET'S GET STARTED. Answer each question honestly, but without too much hemming and hawing. You're only 45 questions away from a new sound and a new life!

(NOTE: Your first invoice is included in this mailing. Payment is due immediately.)

— — — — — — — — — — — —

Your Full Name: **HECTOR THE DUMMY**
Your Handler's Name: **T. Foley**

PART ONE: GENERAL QUESTIONS

1) What are you made of (check all that apply)?
> **_X_ cloth   _X_ wood** __ paper composite **_X_ plastic**

2) Which parts of your body can move?
> **_X_ eyes** __ brows ____ ears **_X_ arms**

3) What is the name of your "Act"?
> **Ventwittoquisms, or "Hector Can't Talk"**

4) What sorts of things does s/he make you say? Please quote him/**her** a few times here:
- **Put me down! Stop putting words into my mouth!**
- **Wanna see the sexiest part of me?**
- **I am a fifty-three-year-old male looking for a lady to ride in my truck on short trips.**

- **I find kissing a great way to reduce stress.**

PART TWO: MULTIPLE CHOICE

5) Where do you think your handler's voice comes from?
- his/her heart
- his/her throat
- his/her terrible childhood
- **somebody else**
- all of the above

6) Which "dummy trope" best describes your persona?
- The Cheeky Boy
- The Hayseed Soldier
- The Grumpy Old Man
- The Lecherous Spinster
- **OTHER** (please elaborate): **None. [I don't care for dummy tropes.]**

7) Which voice do you feel is your closest ancestor?
- **A Greek Sybil, drunk on fumes and spilling the secrets of the Fates**
- A pika, the North American rat known to ward off prey by throwing its voice
- Mister Potter's Humble Voice-in-a-Trunk
- Punch
- Judy

8) Which classic on-screen plot feels closest to your own emotional landscape?

- An obsessive vaudevillian, desperate to give his crowd the perfect performance, practices so much with his dummy that he loses sight of his own personality and goes insane.

- Because of lousy report card grades, a cheeky boy dummy is forbidden to go on a vacation to Sweden with his handler. He stows away on the ocean liner anyway, but he is just too sassy and cute to stay angry with for long.

- The papers for the world's most dangerous nuclear weapon are stashed in the head of a nightclub dummy. The dummy's unsuspecting handler is then set on a madcap transcontinental caper full of song and dance.

- A shy ventriloquist uses his dummy to get girls—and to kill those girls' jealous husbands when they find out the ventriloquist is schtupping their wives.

- **A curly-haired ventriloquist named Dave and his dummy, Danny, land a slot on the <u>Flip Wilson Show</u>. Dave buys them matching red jackets and bowties, but forgets to rehearse. Throughout the act, when Danny speaks, Dave's lips move. When Danny says "no," Dave shakes his head. When they try the ol' cigarette bit, Dave drops Danny while fumbling in his pocket for a lighter. Danny's plastic body hits the stage floor with a thud.**

9) Which famous dummy catchphrase would sound best in your throat?
   - "On a stick!"
   - **"S'alright." [I'm pretty agreeable]**
   - "Tim-berrrrrr!"
   - "I'll clip ya! So help me, I'll mow ya down!"
   - "Diff-eee-cult for you; eeeee-zeee for me."
   - OTHER (please elaborate):

10) Which of the following speeches most intrigues you?
- Richard Milhous Nixon's "Checkers" address
- Sally Field's 1985 Oscar acceptance speech
- The list of the possible side effects of Cialis
- **"Friends, Romans, Countrymen"**
- Vincent Price's rap at the end of "Thriller"

PART THREE: TRUE OR FALSE

11) When I close my eyes, I hear a voice inside my head.   T   **F**

                                    `[I can't close my eyes]`

12) Often, that internal voice is making fun of me.   T   **F**

13) I would like to have a dummy of my own.   **T**   F

14) I would dress my dummy exactly like myself.   T   **F**

15) I would never, ever show the dummy to my handler.   T   **F**

PART FOUR: THE VOCAL SPECTRUM

Rate your feelings regarding each statement, 10 being "strong agreement" and 1 being "total disagreement."

16) I enjoy being looked at by large crowds of people.

            1 2 3 4 5 6 7 8 9 **10**

17) I enjoy speaking to them (through my handler) while they look at me.

            1 2 3 4 5 6 7 8 9 10

18) I agree with the sentiment "loose lips sink ships."

            1 2 3 4 5 6 7 8 9 **10**

19) I often fantasize about calling in to those radio political talk shows.

            1 2 3 4 5 6 7 8 9 10

20) I get emotional during the musical numbers of all four Muppet movies.

1 2 3 4 5 6 7 8 9 10

21) Classical soliloquies have little to no real-life use.

1 2 3 4 5 6 7 8 9 10

22) I envy talking dolls, even though they can only say a few phrases again and again.

1 2 3 4 5 6 7 8 9 **10**

PART FIVE: FILL IN THE BLANKS

23) When I give a performance, it makes me feel **manipulated**.

24) When my handler speaks for me, the sensation is most similar to **plagiarism**

25) If I were to enter a televised singing contest, my song of choice would be **"I Can't Even Walk Without You Holding My Hand."**

26) If my handler were a dummy, his/**her** catchphrase would be **"Ventriloquism is dead!"**

27) My favorite instrument is **A GPS system.**

28) If my handler knew that I **hated the Muppets**, s/he would never work with me again.

PART SIX: VISUAL ASSOCIATIONS

29) What do the following images remind you of? Write short descriptions beneath each one:

A:

Description: **This is a silhouette of a puppet preparing for a French kiss. People aren't generally aware of this, but most puppets do NOT have movable tongues, which is unfortunate.**

B:

Description: **This is just meta-ventriloquism.**

PART SEVEN: SHORT ESSAY

30) What, in your opinion, are voices for?

To express a need--anguish, isolation, hunger; to cry out for mother's milk. Spanish speaking people have a nice expression, "El que no llora; no mama." Vents would argue differently--voices are for throwing.

31) What is your first memory?

Being pulled out of a box, unwrapped from layers of plastic bubble wrap, and taking my first breath.

32) What did it sound like?

It's kinda like when you've been swimming underwater, holding your breath for a while and then you finally reach the surface. You hear yourself gasping for air and then the whole world opens up to your ears! Have you seen The Little Mermaid?

33) What do you enjoy about your handler's voice?

That it changes, and so I change.

34) If s/he were a dummy, what would you make him/her say?

"Waah! Waaaah! Where is everybody? Feed me!"

35) Describe the last dream you had. Did you speak? If so, what did you speak?

Oh, gosh. It was a nightmare. I was talking to James Lipton on Inside the Actor's Studio, and I was petrified, as usual. Couldn't speak at all. I had to engage with Lipton and the audience via text messaging. Foley was there. She read my text messages aloud. We totally sucked--ruined the whole fuckin' episode.

•

PART EIGHT: WORD ASSOCIATION

Read the following words. As you read, quickly type the first word that comes into your head:

36) secret: **DESIRE**

37) strangle: **ME**

38) gimmick: **NO!**

39) orphan: **ME**

40) soft: **LAP**

41) headache: **NO!**

42) Pinocchio: **DADDY DADDY**

43) tether: **POLE**

44) suitcase: **(ho)ME**

——

PART EIGHT: CATCH-ALL

Is there anything else we need to know about you? If so, please write it in the space below.

According to Foley, I have a severe anxiety disorder—selective mutism, so I don't like the idea of speaking in public and/or around strangers.

END of questionnaire!
Congratulations, **HECTOR.** Great work!

Thursday, December 8, 2011

Dear **HECTOR THE DUMMY**:

After painstaking analysis, our experts have reached a conclusion regarding your vocal needs. Based on your answers, **HECTOR**, you require a **Thy-Ro-Id**, or "Thirsty-Romantic-Idealist" voice. This is one of the most complicated vocal types in our catalogue, as it is rife with contradictions.

In our experience, Thy-Ro-Id voice types speak with both a lust for life and an overarching wariness toward it. They are curious and independent thinkers that often find themselves silenced by stronger personalities or by self-doubt. To compensate for this contradiction, they will hide behind the voices and identities of others in both personal and professional capacities.

FAMOUS THY-RO-IDs INCLUDE:

- Frederik, Crown Prince of Denmark
- Tenzing Norgay
- Mel Blanc
- Motown bassist James Jamerson
- John Cazale
- Gerald Ford

We specifically suggest you consider the Thy-Ro-Id voices in our catalogue that blend bombast with meticulousness (catalogue numbers TRI33-50). This will allow you to express your psychic reluctance to perform, while still giving your sound enough razzle-dazzle to land a memorable punch line.

Details and add-ons that will optimize your speaking power:

- We recommend a baritone voice that ends its consonants softly, in the back palate, which will compliment your diminutive stature.

- A melodious dialect, like our "Country Gentleman" (TRI51) or our "Casbah Millionaire" (TRI35.5) add-ons, will give you a bump in status, sonically speaking. This upgrade can also address both your confidence issues *and* your interest in French kissing!

- To compensate for your urges to self-strangulate, we believe the less throaty the resonance you choose, the better. Opt for a chesty or nasally voice, depending on the type of stage work you pursue.

- Your (alarming) hatred of Muppets suggests that a cartoony voice will not work for you. For this reason, we strongly suggest finishing off your Thy-Ro-Id catalogue selection with our "James Earl Jones Varnish" (see "Finishing Touches" in the back of the catalogue), a protective vocal coat that will give you gravitas and much-needed confidence.

All-in-all, **HECTOR**, we are looking forward to helping you blend all these elements of speaking into a perfect vocal cocktail—a voice you can call your own. We do, however, have one small caveat, which we extend to all our clients.

We assume that you view your years on your handler's lap, forced to live in what you call "selective mutism," as the ultimate in manipulation. You probably also feel that, once you have a voice of your own installed into your throat, you will finally be in control of how the world hears you. You're probably thinking that you will never feel puppetted again.

Unfortunately, though, **HECTOR**, a man's voice is his *ultimate* puppeteer. If we have learned anything from our decades of vocal study, it is that when you abide such a complicated organ, you are more likely to fall prey to it then you are to master it.

Sometimes it will be an unruly little man on your knee, undermining your patter and stealing your best jokes. Your listeners' attention will gravitate to it, even though you are the one who wrote the material. But other times, *you* will be the unruly little man, and it will feel as though the voice has its hand up your back and is jerking your body into places without asking permission.

But oh, it will sound very pretty at times. It will be able to leap farther than you yourself can leap, and it will draw people close to you from unimaginable distances. You will see people's eyes widen with alarm when it sends out a vigorous yell.

We must insist that you at least try to trust your new voice, as often, it will know better than you do. You should listen to it heckle from within, and you should follow it when it pulls the strings of your body in unexpected directions. For its choices are usually deep and telling, even if they trouble you as they manifest themselves. Whether you admit it or not (and some never do), the voice is the closest you will ever get to showing an audience what you are truly made of.

But make no mistake about it, **HECTOR**: in this new act of your career, that voice inside you will always be the straight man, and you will forever be its yutz.

GOOD LUCK!

The Amputee

HELLO. THIS IS MY FIRST VIDEO.

UNFORTUNATELY I HAVE A MIC, BUT NO CAMERA, SO YOU CAN'T SEE ME. AS YOU MAY HAVE GUESSED, I ALSO HAVE NO VOICE. MY VOCAL CORDS WERE SURGICALLY REMOVED A FEW YEARS AGO. MY LARYNX AND TRACHEA ARE STILL INTACT, SO I CAN GET AIR INTO MY MOUTH AND MAKE SMALL, NON-VOCAL SOUNDS.

THE SOUND YOU ARE HEARING IS PRODUCED BY SOMETHING CALLED AN ELECTRONIC, OR ARTIFICIAL, LARYNX. I MOUTH MY WORDS WHILE PUSHING A BUTTON AND THIS DEVICE PROVIDES A STEADY BUZZING SOUND SO THAT THE WORDS CAN BE HEARD.

I'LL END BY DEMONSTRATING WHAT I SOUND LIKE WHEN I TRY TO SPEAK WITHOUT THE ARTIFICIAL LARYNX. I'LL PUT DOWN MY DEVICE AND WON'T USE IT AGAIN IN THIS VIDEO. IF YOU WISH TO HEAR WHAT I SOUND LIKE SPEAKING WITHOUT IT, TURN UP YOUR VOLUME. YOU'LL BE ABLE TO HEAR SOME WORDS, BUT NOT ALL. HERE GOES:

NOTES

The play in which I had to say the "Eew" line, and from which I quote in "Playing Sick," is Michael Hollinger's *An Empty Plate in the Café du Grand Boeuf.* I did not cite the play by name in the essay because I didn't want Hollinger's fine script to be immediately connected with so much unrelated angst on my part. Any actor, disgust issues notwithstanding, would be lucky to play Mimi.

Hector the Dummy's responses in "A Monstrous Little Voice" were written by Teresa Foley, the artist responsible for creating him. You can learn more about her—and about Hector—at *http:// ventwittoquisms.tumblr.com/.*

BIBLIOGRAPHY

COMMON SOURCES

Balan, Ronald J. and Robert F. Orlikoff. *Clinical Measurement of Speech and Voice.* 2nd ed. Valley Stream, NY: Singular, 1999.

Karpf, Anne. *The Human Voice.* New York: Bloomsbury, 2006.

Linklater, Kristin. *Freeing the Natural Voice: Imagery and Art in the Practice of Voice and Language.* 2nd ed. Hollywood, CA: Drama Publishers, 2006.

Milner, Greg. *Perfecting Sound Forever: An Aural History of Recorded Music.* New York: Faber and Faber, 2009.

Sataloff, Robert Thayer. "The Professional Voice Part III: Common Diagnoses and Treatments. *Journal of Voice* 1, no. 3 (1987): 283–92. doi10.1016/S0892-1997(87)80014-0.

Saturday Night Live: The Complete First Season. 26 hours. 1975; New York: Universal Home Video, 2011. DVD.

Schecter, Scott. *Judy Garland: The Day-by-Day Chronicle of a Legend.* New York: Taylor Trade, 2006.

Titze, Ingo R. "The Human Instrument." *Scientific American* 298, no. 1 (2008). doi:10.1038 scientificamerican0108-94.

Vaughan, Denis. "Orchestral Sound in Concert Halls." *Musical Times* 122, no. 1657 (1981):67–69. *JSTOR.* http://www.jstor.org/.

DOWN IN THE HOLLER

A Streetcar Named Desire, directed by Elia Kazan. 1951; Burbank, CA: Warner Home Video, 2006. DVD.

THE STARLET

King Kong, directed by Merian C. Cooper. 1 hour. 1933; New York: Turner Home Entertainment, 2006. DVD.

THE WILHELM SCREAM

A Star is Born. Directed by George Cukor. 2 hours. 1954; Burbank, CA: Warner Home Video, 2000. DVD.

Carpenter, Jeffrey. Interview by author. Telephone. October 17, 2006.

"*Charge at Feather River* (1953)." Internet Movie Database. Last modified November 24, 2011. http://www.imdb.com/title/tt0045621.

Demme, Joeseph. "Complete List of Wilhelm Screams." Cinexcellence. Last modified June 25, 2011. http://www.cinexcellence .com/2011/05/complete-list-of-wilhelm-screams.

Distant Drums. Directed by Raoul Walsh. 1 hour. 1951; Studio City, CA: Republic Pictures, 2004. DVD.

"History of the Wilhelm Scream." Hollywood Lost and Found. Retrieved November 8, 2006, from http://www.youtube.com/ watch?v=_PxALy22utc.

Kendall, Alan. *David Garrick: A Biography.* London: Harrap, 1985.

Lee, James. "Cue the Scream: Meet Hollywood's Go-to Shriek." *Wired,* Sept. 25, 2007. http://www.wired.com/.

Pucinni, Giacomo. *Tosca.* Coro e Orchestra del Teatro alla Scala di Milano. Conducted by Victor de Sabata. EMI Classics compact disc 0724356289321.

Thank You for Smoking. Directed by Jason Reitman. 1.5 hours. 2005; Century City, CA: Fox Searchlight Pictures, 2006. DVD.

The Wild Bunch: Original Director's Cut. Directed by Sam Peckinpah. 2 hours. 1969; Burbank, CA: Warner Home Video, 2006. DVD.

"The Wilhelm Scream." Hollywood Lost and Found. Last modified May 1, 2010. http://hollywoodlostandfound.net/wilhelm/index.html.

THE MOTOR-MOUTH

Mast, Joseph. Interview by author. Telephone. December 7, 2011.

HOW TO SPELL THE REBEL YELL

Akers, Monte. "The Rebel Yell." The Stonewall Brigade. Last modified December 31, 2008. http://www.stonewallbrigade.com/articles _rebelyell.html.

Bierce, Ambrose. "A Little of Chickamauga." *Phantoms of a Blood-stained Period: The Complete Civil War Writings of Ambrose Bierce.* Edited by Russell Duncan and David J. Klooster. Amherst: University of Massachusetts Press, 2002.

The Crystals. "He's a Rebel." *Da Doo Ron Ron: The Very Best of the Crystals.* Sony Legacy compact disc 761288.

The Civil War, directed by Ken Burns. 10 hours. PBS Home Video, 2002. DVD.

Davis, Donald A. *Stonewall Jackson: Lessons in Leadership.* New York: Palgrave Macmillan, 2007.

Faulkner, William. *Light in August.* 1932. Reprint, New York: Vintage, 1990.

Foote, Shelby. *Fort Sumter to Perryville.* Vol. 1 of *The Civil War.* New York: Vintage, 1986.

Fremantle, Arthur James Lyon, Sir. *The Fremantle Diary.* Edited by Walter Lord. 1954. Reprint, New York: Capricorn Books, 1960.

"*Gone With the Wind*: Atlanta Premiere Stirs South to Tears and Cheers." *Life,* December 25, 1939: 9. Google Books. http://books.google .com.

Goolrick, Chester. "WAH-WHO-EEE." *The New Yorker,* June 16, 1956: 59–60. http://www.newyorker.com/archive/.

Idol, Billy. "Rebel Yell." *Rebel Yell.* Chrysalis FV compact disc 41450.

Johnson, James Weldon. *Autobiography of an Ex-colored Man.* 1912. Reprint, Minneapolis: Filiquarian, 2007.

Keegan, John, ed. *The Book of War: 25 Centuries of Great War Writing.* New York: Penguin, 2000.

McGowan, Stanley S. "The Rebel Yell." *Encyclopedia of the American Civil War.* Edited by David Stephen Heidler, Jeanne T. Heidler, and David J. Coles. New York: Norton, 2000.

Mitchell, Margaret. *Gone With the Wind.* 1936. Reprint, New York: Scribner, 2011.

Petty, Tom. "Rebels." *Southern Accents.* MCA compact disc 5486.

Public Enemy. "Black Steel in the Hour of Chaos." *It Takes a Nation of Millions to Hold Us Back.* Def Jam 527 compact disc 38–2.

Read, Allen Walker. "The Rebel Yell as a Linguistic Problem." *American Speech* 36, no. 2 (1961): 83–92. Communication and Mass Media Complete 9650834.

Russell, William Howard. *My Diary North and South.* Edited by Eugene H. Berwanger. Baton Rouge: LSU Press, 2001.

Smith, H. Allen. "I Tracked Down the Rebel Yell." *Saturday Evening Post,* December 6, 1952. 36 & 153.

"Thomas Alexander's Rebel Yell." Society for the Historical Preservation of the 26th Regiment, North Carolina. Accessed November

25, 2011. http://www.26nc.org/History/Rebel-Yell/Sound-Files/ RebelYell_l.wav.

Webster's Online Dictionary, s.v. "Battle cry (extended definition)." Accessed November 23, 2011. http://www.websters-online-dictionary.org/.

Whitman, Walt. *Specimen Days*. 1882. Reprint, Mineola: Dover, 1995.

Wormser, Richard. "Red Summer." *Jim Crow Stories*. PBS. Last modified 2002. http://www.pbs.org/wnet/jimcrow/stories_events_red.html.

THE CANDIDATE

Peduto, Bill. Interview by author. Telephone. September 15, 2011.

COMMUNICATION BREAKDOWN

"ABC NEWS: 'Oops!' A Mea Culpa on the 'Dean Scream' Coverage." *Winning Back America*. http://www.winningbackamerica.com/ weblog/weblogs/index.html.

Bauder, David. "CNN Says It Overplayed Dean's Iowa Scream." The Associated Press, February 8, 2004. http://www.ap.org/.

"Clinton's Angry Response to Heckler" (Video 2006). Retrieved November 25, 2011, from http://www.youtube.com/watch?v= JGTQZnC-6a4.

"Dean's Iowa Speech Looms over Him." The Associated Press. January 21, 2004. http://www.ap.org/.

Dickerson, John. "Presidential Anger Management." *Slate*. June 10, 2010. http://www.slate.com/articles/news_and_politics/politics/ 2010/06/presidential_anger_management.html.

"Do the Iowa Caucus Results Change Dean's Status Among the Candidates? (Poll)" *Time*, January 20, 2004. http://www.time.com/.

"Gore Campaign Chooses Rock Songs." ABC News. August 16, 2000. http://abcnews.go.com/.

Gourevitch, Philip. "The Shakeout." *The New Yorker*. February 9, 2004, 28–33. http://www.newyorker.com/archive/.

"Howard and Judy Dean: The Diane Sawyer Interview." Crocuta's Political Produce. January 22, 2004. http://www.crocuta.net/Dean/Transcript _of_Diane_Sawyer_Interview.htm.

"Howard Dean's Scream" Video (2006). Retrieved November 25, 2011, from http://www.youtube.com/watch?v=D5FzCeV0ZFc.

"Howard Dean's Scream—the Original" Video (2010). Retrieved

November 25, 2011, from http://www.youtube.com/watch?v=-3 Meg3CEyUM.

"John Rich Writes McCain Campaign Song." *The Boot.* August 1, 2008. http://www.theboot.com/.

Keefer, Bryan. "Tsunami." *Columbia Journalism Review* 43, no.2 (2004): 18–23.

Leland, John. "Nice Campaign, But Can We Dance to It?" *New York Times.* July 11, 2004. http://www.nytimes.com/.

Lublin, Joann S. "The Hoarse Race: When Candidates Lose Their Voices." *Wall Street Journal.* January 25, 2008. http://online.wsj.com/.

Marinucci, Carla. "Iowa Yell Stirring Doubts About Dean." *San Francisco Gate.* January 21, 2004. http://www.sfgate.com/.

Meyer, Dick. "Defending Dean's Scream." CBS News. January 23, 2004. http://www.cbsnews.com/.

"Poll: 3 of 4 Think Our Most Trusted Presidents Have Lied." CNN. February 22, 2010. http://articles.cnn.com/.

"Reagan's Nashua Moment" Video (2008). Retrieved November 25, 2011, from http://www.youtube.com/watch?v=OO2_49TycdE.

Schweitzer, Sarah. "Yell in Iowa May Haunt Dean Camp." *Boston Globe.* January 21, 2004. http://www.boston.com/.

Shapiro, Walter. "In Iowa, Raw Emotion and an Anything-Can-Happen Feeling." *USA Today.* January 18, 2004. http://www.usatoday.com/.

Shields, Mark. "Democrats Owe a Debt to Dean." CNN. January 29, 2004. http://www.cnn.com/.

Suddath, Claire. "A Brief History of Campaign Songs." *Time.* Accessed November 25, 2011. http://www.time.com/time/specials/packages/article/0,28804,1840981_1840998_1840943,00.html.

Thibault, David. "Kerry Climbing, Dean Dwindling in NH." *CNS News.* July 7, 2008. http://cnsnews.com/.

Walsh, Kenneth T. "The Battle Cry That Backfired on Howard 'The Scream' Dean." *US News & World Report.* January 17, 2008. http://www.usnews.com/.

York, Byron. "Dean Loses It." *National Review.* January 20, 2004. http://old.nationalreview.com/.

THE ZEALOT

Stelling, Edward R. "I Spoke in Tongues (1970)." SOA Web Ministries. Accessed November 15, 2011. http://soamc.org/.

HARPY

"A Desire to Shout for Stella." Video (2011). Retrieved November 25, 2011, from http://www.youtube.com/watch?v=rAStu4dxMiw.

McKenna, Sheila. Interview by author. Telephone. May 4, 2011.

Miller, Arthur. *The Crucible.* 1952. Reprint, New York: Dramatists Play Service, 1994.

Owen, Paul. Interview by author. Internet chat. August 10, 2010.

Payne, Matthew. Interview by author. Telephone. May 7, 2011.

"Stella Finals 2008." Video (2008). Retrieved November 25, 2011, from http://www.youtube.com/watch?v=fbyNG2ilhrI&feature=related.

"Stella Shout Out New Orleans Tennessee Williams Festival 2009." Video (2009). Retrieved November 25, 2011, from http://www.youtube.com/watch?v=UPqyvg14HTY.

Williams, Tennessee. *A Streetcar Named Desire.* 1947. Reprint, New York: Signet, 1986.

"Yay! A Girl Is the Winner of the 2011 Stella Shouting Contest in New Orleans!" Video (2011). Retrieved November 25, 2011, from http://www.youtube.com/watch?v=r-b6BZwfahw.

THE NOVICE

Miller, Jane. Interview by author. Telephone. August 26, 2011.

SPACE ODDITY

Cohen, John. *Mountain Music of Peru.* Smithsonian Folkways compact disc 40020.

Sagan, Carl, et al. *Murmurs of Earth: The Voyager Interstellar Record.* New York: Random House, 1978.

Saturday Night Live: The Complete Third Season. 22.5 hours. Universal Home Video, 2011. DVD.

Voyager Golden Record. NASA. Accessed November 25, 2011. http://goldenrecord.org/.

"Voyager: The Interstellar Mission." California Institute of Technology Jet Propulsion Laboratory. Accessed November 25, 2011. http://voyager.jpl.nasa.gov/spacecraft/goldenrec.html.

THE SOPRANO

Wolfe, Carol. Interview by author. Telephone. February 8, 2007.

JUDY! JUDY! JUDY!

Bliven, Bruce. "Annals of Architecture: A Better Sound." *The New Yorker*, November 8, 1976. http://www.newyorker.com/.

Bruce, Lenny. *Lenny Bruce: Live at the Curran Theater*. Fantasy 34201, vinyl disc.

Carnegie Hall. Carnegie Hall Corporation. Accessed November 28, 2011. http://www.carnegiehall.org/.

"Carnegie Hall." New York Preservation Archive Project. Last modified 2010. http://www.nypap.org/content/carnegie-hall.

Clarke, Gerald. *Get Happy: The Life of Judy Garland*. New York: Delta, 2000.

Finch, Christopher. *Rainbow: The Stormy Life of Judy Garland*. New York: Grosset and Dunlap, 1975.

Frank E. Campbell Funeral Chapel. "Frank E. Campbell: the Funeral Chapel." Accessed November 28, 2011. http://www.frankecampbell.com/.

Frank, Gerald. *Judy*. Cambridge, MA: Da Capo, 1999.

Fricke, John. *Judy Garland: A Portrait in Art and Anecdote*. Boston: Bullfinch Press, 2003.

Garland, Judy. *Judy at Carnegie Hall: Fortieth Anniversary Edition*. Capitol 27876 compact disc.

Jaffe, J. Christopher. *The Acoustics of Performance Halls*. New York: Norton, 2010.

Kaplan, James. "Over the Rainbow, and Then Some!" *Vanity Fair*, May 2011, 142–49.

"On Concert Halls: Conversations with Ralph Kirkpatrick." *Perspecta* 17 (1980): 92–99. JSTOR. http://www.jstor.org/

Sleaff, Michael T. and Deborah J. Hopster. *Post Mortem Technique Handbook*. New York: Springer, 2005.

THE CONTESTANT

Griffith, Daina. Interview by author. Pittsburgh, PA, June 4, 2011.

HEY BIG SPENDER

"Alessandro Moreschi, The Last Castrato, Ave Maria." Video (2011). Retrieved December 1, 2011, from http://www.youtube.com/watch?v=711ZhavjIO4.

Anastasio, Angelo and Nicholas Bussard. "Mouth Air Pressure and Intensity

Profiles of the Oboe." *Journal of Research in Musical Education* 19, no. 1 (1971): 62–76. JSTOR. http://www.jstor.org/.

Barbier, Patrick. *The World of the Castrati: The History of an Extraordinary Operatic Phenomenon.* London: Souvenir Press, 1998.

Bolig, John Richard. *Caruso Records: A History and Discography.* Denver: Mainspring Press, 2002.

"Caruso Appeal Is Ready; His Singing Not So Sure." *New York Times.* November 25, 1906. http://www.nytimes.com/.

"Caruso Bursts Blood Vessel in Throat." *New York Times.* December 12, 1920. http://www. www.nytimes.com/.

"Caruso Bust in Silver." *New York Times.* April 20, 1911. http://www .nytimes.com/.

Caruso, Enrico. *The Complete Recordings of Enrico Caruso.* Naxos compact disc 8.110703.

"Caruso Sails Today to Be Operated On." *New York Times.* April 14, 1909. http://www.nytimes.com/.

"Caruso Sings to Keep Farms Going." *New York Times.* November 13, 1913. http://www.nytimes.com/.

"Caruso's Injury Serious." *New York Times.* October 13, 1910. http://www .nytimes.com/.

"Castrato Superstar Disinterred." BBC News. July 12, 2006. http://news .bbc.co.uk/.

Celletti, Rodolfo. *A History of Bel Canto.* New York: Oxford University Press USA, 1997.

A Century of Caruso. Edited by Frank Merkling. New York: Metropolitan Opera Guild, 1975.

Clapton, Nicholas. *Moreschi: The Last Castrato.* London: Haus, 2004.

Harris, Ellen T. "Farinelli." Grove Music Online. Accessed February 18, 2008. Oxford Music Online. http://www.oxfordmusiconline.com/.

Jackson, Stanley. *Caruso.* New York: Stein and Day, 1972.

Jenkins, J. S. "The Voice of the Castrato." *The Lancet* 351 (1998): 1825–898. doi:10.1016/S0140-6736(97)10198-2.

"Ranges of Orchestral Instruments." Symphony Orchestral Library. Accessed December 2, 2011. http://www.orchestralibrary.com/ reftables/rang.html.

Rosselli, John. *Singers of Italian Opera.* Cambridge, UK and New York: Cambridge University Press, 1992.

Sacrificium. Cecilia Bartoldi and Il Giardino Armonico, conducted by Giovanni Antonini. Decca compact disc 4781521.

Scott, Michael. *The Great Caruso.* New York: Viking Penguin, 1988.

Secrist, John. *Caruso: His Life in Pictures.* New York: Studio Publications, 1957.

Suisman, David. "Welcome to the Monkey House." *The Believer,* June 2004. http://www.believermag.com/issues/200406/?read=article_suisman.

"With the Aid of a Tambor Machine, We May All Become Carusos." *New York Times.* December 20, 1908. http://www.nytimes.com/.

THE PHOENIX

Zollo, David. Interview by author. Iowa City, IA. November 20, 2007.

AND YOUR BIRD CAN SING

"A Murder of Crows (Video)." *Nature.* PBS. October 24, 2011. http://www.pbs.org/wnet/nature/episodes/a-murder-of-crows/full-episode/5977/.

"*Billboard* Magazine Archives." *Billboard.* Last Modified November 2011. http://www.billboard.com/archive/.

Bluff, Lucas A., Alex Kacelnik, Christian Rutz. "Vocal Culture in New Caledonian Crows." *Biological Journal of the Linnean Society* 101, no. 4 (December 2010): 767-776. doi: 10.1111/j.1095-8312.2010.01527.

Brown, Eleanor D. "The Role of Song and Vocal Imitation among Common Crows." *Ethology* 68, no. 2 (1985): 115–36. doi: 10.1111/j.1439-0310.1985.tb00119.

———. *The Song of the Common Crow.* College Park: University of Maryland Press, 1979.

Chamberlain, Dwight R. and George W. Cornwell. "Selected Vocalizations of the Common Crow." *The Auk* 88, no. 3 (1971). doi: 10.1111/j.1095-8312.2010.01527.

The Fendermen. "Muleskinner Blues." *Goofy Greats.* K-Tel NU 9030, MP3.

"The Story of the Fendermen." The Fendermen. Accessed December 1, 2011. http://www.fendermen.com/history/history.html.

"Gee—The Crows: Electronic Stereo Version." Video (2010). Retrieved December 1, 2011, from http://www.youtube.com/watch?v=lzxO_pO1ZpI.

Ghosh, Pallab. "'Oldest Musical Instrument' Found." BBC News. June 25, 2009. http://news.bbc.co.uk/.

Marler, Peter. Nature's Music: *The Science of Birdsong*. Waltham, MA: Academic Press, 2004.

Marler, Peter and Doupe, Allison. "Singing in the Brain." PNAS 97, no. 7 (March 2000). doi: 10.1073/pnas.97.7.2965.

No Direction Home. Directed by Martin Scorsese. 3 hours. Los Angeles, CA: Paramount Pictures, 2005. DVD.

Rogers, Lesley J. and Gisela Kaplan. *Songs, Roars, and Rituals: Communication in Birds, Mammals and Other Animals*. Cambridge, MA: Harvard University Press, 2000.

Sagar, Keith. *The Laughter of Foxes: A Study of Ted Hughes*. 2nd ed. Liverpool: Liverpool University Press, 2000.

THE KING

Roberts, Donnie. Interview by author. Telephone. September 7, 2011.

TEACH ME TONIGHT

"'82 Tonys—*Dreamgirls*' 'And I Am Telling You I'm Not Going,'" VIDEO (2006). Retrieved

December 1, 2011, from http://www.youtube.com/watch?v=kC_u_q-iND0.

"Buddy Holly—'Peggy Sue' (Arthur Murray Dance Party 1957)," Video (2009). Retrieved December 1, 2011, from http://www.youtube.com/watch?v=XDP4l7wN4CE.

"Cartoon Swooner Crooner from Looney Tunes." Video (2010). Retrieved December 1, 2011, from http://www.youtube.com/watch?v=Whi0b1ZEoa0.

The Crickets. *The 'Chirping' Crickets*. 1957. Universal compact disc 31182.

Dorsey, Jimmy. *Jimmy Dorsey Plays His Greatest Hits*. Deluxe Records GCD 1003, compact disc.

Dorsey, Tommy. *The Best of Tommy Dorsey*. Bluebird/ RCA compact disc 51087-2.

"Episode 13: Smokey Robinson." *Elvis Costello Spectacle, Season One*. Directed by Dave Russell. 10 hours. New York: Video Service Corp, 2009. DVD.

"Frank Sinatra Album and Chart History." *Billboard*. Accessed December 1, 2011. http://www.billboard.com/artist/frank-sinatra/chart-history/3626#/artist/frank-sinatra/chart-history/3626.

Frank Sinatra: Concert Collection, directed by Dwight Hemion. 14 hours. Los Angeles: Shout Factory, 2010. DVD.

"Frank Sinatra, 'Strangers in the Night' 1994." Video (2011). Retrieved December 1, 2011, from http://www.youtube.com/watch?v =MMY3HATbdvw.

Holden, Stephen. "Frank Sinatra Opens and Then Cancels." *New York Times*. May 17, 1990. http://www.nytimes.com/.

Jacobs, George and William Stadiem. *Mr S.: My Life With Sinatra*. New York: Harper Collins, 2004.

Jerry Lee Lewis: Greatest Live Performances of the 50s, 60s, and 70s. 1 hour. Los Angeles: Time Life Records, 2007. DVD.

Kaplan, James. *Frank: The Voice*. New York: Doubleday, 2010. Kindle Edition.

Kelly, Kitty. *His Way: An Unauthorized Biography of Frank Sinatra*. New York: Bantam, 1987.

Lewis, Jerry Lee. *Jerry Lee Lewis*. Rhino compact disc R270656.

Little Richard. *Here's Little Richard*. Universal compact disc 31182.

Popular Song. Popular Song. Last modified July 2011. Accessed December 2, 2011. http://www.popularsong.org/.

Porterfield, Nolan. *Jimmie Rodgers*. Urbana and Chicago: University of Illinois Press, 1992.

Sinatra, Frank. *Frank Sinatra Sings for Only the Lonely*. Capitol compact disc 7484712.

———. *Songs for Young Lovers/Swing Easy*. Capitol compact disc 96089.

———. *The Very Best of Frank Sinatra*. Reprise compact disc 946589-2.

Sinatra, Frank and John Quinlan. "Tips on Popular Singing." 1941. Jazz Singers. Accessed December 1, 2011. http://www.jazzsingers. com/TipsOnPopularSinging/.

Summers, Anthony and Robbyn Swan. *Sinatra: The Life*. New York: Vintage, 2005.

Talese, Gay. "Frank Sinatra Has a Cold." *The Gay Talese Reader: Portraits and Encounters*. New York: Walker and Company, 2003.

THE FRONTMAN

Meadows, Robert. Interview by author. Telephone. November 29, 2011.

THE INTERPRETER
Star, Joy. Interview by author. Telephone, October 31, 2007.

PLEASE HOLD
Cocteau, Jean. *La Voix Humaine*. 1930. New York: Samuel French, 1992.
The Human Voice. Directed by Ted Kotcheff. 1966. West Long Branch, NJ: Kultur, 2002. DVD.
Huurdeman, Anton A. *The Worldwide History of Telecommunications*. Hoboken, NJ: Wiley and Sons, 2003.
Kramare, Chris. *Keeping in Touch: Technology and Women's Voices*. New York: Methuen, 1998.
"Telephone Ads Through the Decades." *Crooked Brains*. August 23, 2007. http://www.crookedbrains.net/.

THE ILLUSIONIST
Watt, William J. Interview by author. Telephone. November 17, 2011.

DOUBLE JOY: MYRON COPE AND THE PITTSBURGH SOUND
"Barbara Johnstone Lecture: Pittsburghese." Video (2008). Retrieved December 5, 2011, from http://www.youtube.com/watch?v=H8ihyTbi2Kw.
Collier, Gene. "Obituary: Myron Cope's Career Spanned Newspapers, Magazines, Radio and TV." *Pittsburgh Post-Gazette*, February 27, 2008. http://www.post-gazette.com/.
Cope, Myron. *Double Yoi!* Champaign, IL: Sports Publishing, 2002.
"Copeisms." Arlin's Myron Cope Sounds. Accessed December 3, 2011. http://www.steelerbear.com/psfcom/myron/copeism.html.
Johnstone, Barbara. "Pittsburghese Shirts: Commodification and the Enregisterment of an Urban Dialect. *American Speech* 84, no. 2 (2009): 157–75. doi: 10.1215/00031283-2009-013.
Johnstone, Barbara, Jennifer Andrus and Andrew E. Danielson. "Mobility, Indexicality, and the Enregisterment of 'Pittsburghese.'" *Journal of English Linguistics* 34, no. 2 (2006): 77–104. doi: 10.1177/0075424206290692.
Johnstone, Barbara and Andrew Danielson. "'Pittsburghese' in the Daily Papers, 1910–2001: Historical Sources of Ideology about Variation." Presentation at the 30th annual conference on New Ways of Analyzing Variation (NWAV 30), Raleigh, NC, October 11–14, 2001.

Johnstone, Barbara and Scott Keisling. "American Varieties: Steeltown Speech." *PBS.* Last modified 2005. http://www.pbs.org/speak/ seatosea/americanvarieties/pittsburghese/. Accessed December 2, 2011.

McCool, Sam. *Sam McCool's New Pittsburghese: How to Speak Like a Pittsburgher.* Pittsburgh, PA: Hayford, 1982.

Pittsburgh Speech and Society. University of Pittsburgh. Last modified 2011. Accessed December 2, 2011. http://pittsburghspeech.pitt .edu/.

Sultan, Tim. "It's Not the Sights, It's the Sounds." *New York Times.* March 17, 2006. http://nytimes.com/.

Templeton, David. "Steelers Fans Toast Myron Cope." *Pittsburgh Post-Gazette,* January 24, 2011. http://www.post-gazette.com/.

THE ILLUSTRATOR

"Joe Starkey's Call of the 1982 Cal-Stanford Big Game's Final Play." *Sign On San Diego.* November 14, 2002. http://www.signonsandiego.com/.

PLAYING SICK

Darwin, Charles. *The Expression of the Emotions in Man and Animals.* 1872. Reprint, New York: New York University Press, 1989.

Desmond, Adrian and James Moore. *Darwin: The Life of a Tormented Evolutionist.* New York: Norton, 1994.

Haidt, John, Clark McCauley, and Paul Rozin. "Disgust." *Handbook of Emotions.* Edited by M. Lewis and J. Haviland. New York: Guilford Press, 1993.

————. "The Disgust Scale (Revised)." The Disgust Scale Home Page. Last modified May 30, 2011. http://people.virginia.edu/~jdh6n/ disgustscale.html.

Hollinger, Michael. *An Empty Plate in the Café du Grand Boeuf.* New York: Dramatists Play Service, 2003.

Miller, Susan B. *Disgust: The Gatekeeper Emotion.* Hillsdale, NJ: Analytic Press, 2004.

Miller, William I. *The Anatomy of Disgust.* Cambridge, MA: Harvard University Press, 1997.

Neuhause, Cable. "When He Can Teach Children to Say 'Yuk,' Dr. Richard Moriarty Ends the Danger of Infant Poisoning." *People,* April 9, 1979. http://www.people.com/.

"Paris at Last," directed by James V. Kern. *I Love Lucy, the Complete Fifth Season.* 11 hours. 1956. Hollywood, CA: CBS Video, 2004. DVD.

Wilson, R. Rawdon. *The Hydra's Tale: Imagining Disgust.* Edmonton, AB: University of Alberta Press, 2002.

THE SHAPE-SHIFTER

Meskimen, Jim. Interview by author. Telephone. August 22, 2011.

A MONSTROUS LITTLE VOICE

"Albert Brooks Ventriloquist Bit." Video (2010). Retrieved December 8, 2011, from http://www.youtube.com/watch?v=_J43bcbIzfI.

Asbury, Kelly. *Dummy Days: America's Favorite Ventriloquists from Radio and Early TV.* Santa Monica, CA: Angel City Press, 2003.

Bergen, Edgar. *How to Become a Ventriloquist.* 1938. Mineola, NY: Dover Press, 2000.

Connor, Steven. *Dumbstruck: A Cultural History of Ventriloquism.* Oxford and New York: Oxford University Press, 2000.

Dolar, Mladen. *A Voice and Nothing More.* Cambridge, MA: MIT Press, 2006.

Vox, Valentine. *I Can See Your Lips Moving: The History and Art of Ventriloquism.* North Hollywood, CA: Plato Publishing, 1993.

THE AMPUTEE

"Speaking Without Vocal Cords." Video (2006). Retrieved October 16, 2007, from http://www.youtube.com/watch?v=_9odHL0MhaM.

ACKNOWLEDGMENTS

I owe so much to Sarah Gorham, who backed this project from an early stage, and to the rest of Sarabande, who turned these essays into a real-live book.

Many thanks to The MacDowell Colony, the Bread Loaf Writers Conference, the Hambidge Center for the Arts, and the University of Iowa Museum of Art for giving me funding, space, and camaraderie.

Thanks also to the journals in which earlier (and sometimes quite different) versions of these essays appeared: *New Madrid, Gulf Coast, Normal School, Iowa Review, Superstition Review,* and *Creative Nonfiction's Pittsburgh in Words* anthology.

In putting these essays together, I often bugged unsuspecting friends, both over the Internet and in frantic cell phone missives. Dozens of people responded with contacts or facts or translations, so thank you to that big crowd for so many little assists.

Other friends offered major info, advice, shelter, or pep talks, and I can't thank them enough. I'm looking at you, Jane Miller, Carol Wolfe, Daina Griffith, Sheila McKenna, Bill Watt, Patrick Jordan, David Conrad, Paul K. Owen, Alexi Morrissey, Jim Ruland, Rachel Gilbert, Matthew G. and Louisa Frank, Christinjamin Drevlolson, Tomás Q. Morin, W. Todd Kaneko, Caitlin Horrocks, and Ben and Sharon VanderWilp.

And thank goodness for my patient teachers and schoolmates, who helped with early drafts and more: Riley Hanick, Ryan Van Meter, Ashley Butler, T. Fleischmann, Nick Kowalczyk, April Freely, David Hamilton, Susan Lohafer, Jeff Porter, and Mary Ruefle.

Vociferous thanks to John D'Agata.

Caroline Casey is a shrewd reader, a Herculean friend, and the best hypeman this side of *Terror Dome*-era Flava Flav. I am wicked grateful for her.

David Turkel, as with most things in my life, had my back through every neutrino of this process. It is not enough to say that I am grateful for him. I am a total Jeepster for him.

I promised several people that I would not thank my cats.

ELENA PASSARELLO

is an actor and writer originally from Charleston, SC. She studied nonfiction at the University of Pittsburgh and the University of Iowa, and her essays have appeared in *Creative Nonfiction, Gulf Coast, Slate, Iowa Review, Normal School, Literary Bird Journal, Ninth Letter,* and in the music writing anthology *Pop When the World Falls Apart.* She has performed in several regional theaters in the East and Midwest, originating roles in the premieres of Christopher Durang's *Mrs. Bob Cratchit's Wild Christmas Binge* and David Turkel's *Wild Signs* and *Holler.* In 2011, she became the first woman to win the annual Stella Screaming Contest in New Orleans.